Phil's

Ph'riends' & Ph'amily's Ph'avorite Recipes!

Created and Compiled by

Staige Ph'amily Members & Ph'riends

All profits from the sale of this book go to the Phil Staige Benefit Fund

Produced & Published by
Nasus Publishing • PO Box 641
Minneapolis, MN 55372

Contents of this book is a compilation of favorite recipes gathered from numerous contributors in support of this fundraiser,. Origins of most of the recipes are unknown. Unless otherwise noted, contributors do not claim to have developed these recipes themselves, only that they remain favorites in their respective households, or have adapted old standards into new favorites.

Library of Congress Control Number: Applied for
Printed in the United States of America
ISBN: 0-0670291-4-7

Table of Contents for Ph'abulous Recipes

Appetizers, Dips & Ruin-Your-Appetite Starters

Ph'abulous Creamy Dip with Toasted Pecan 17
Bacon-Ph'illed Cherry Tomatoes 18
Do Ahead Cheese Puffs 19
Jack Daniels Honey Mustard Glazed Ribs 20
Baked Potato Chips 21
Chicken Wings 22
Pesto Shrimp Pizza Bites 23
Crab Stuffed Mushrooms 24
Wonton Appetizers 25
Wonton Dipping Chips 26
Taco Dip 27
Hot Artichoke Dip and Crackers 28

Salads, Slaws & I-Want-A-Second-Helping Side Dishes

Curried Chicken Salad 31
Orange Fluff 32
Mushroom Corn Casserole 33
Grandma's 24 Hour Salad 34
Barbecued Bean Salad 35
Marketplace Salad 36
Chinese Noodle Salad 37
Seasoned Unfried Ph'rench Ph'ries 38

Pasta Salad 39
Calico Beans 40
Calico Beans II 41
Super Pasta and Vegetable Salad 42
Artichoke Rice Salad 43
Bev's Pasta Salad 44
Joyce Farrell's Ph'ruit Salad Dressing 45
Pico de Gallo 46
Billie's Spinach Salad 47
Hash Brown Cheese Potatoes 48
Copper Penny's 49
Jo Shipleys Cucumbers 50
Billy's Poppy Lime Dressing 51
Poppy Seed Dressing for Ph'ruit 52
Leaf Lettuce with Buttermilk Dressing 53
Exotic Chicken Salad 54
Cherry Pie Ph'illing Salad 55
Our Ph'amily's Ph'avorite Cole Slaw 56
Chinese Chicken Salad 57
'Hold-the-Eggs & Anchovies' Caesar Salad 58
Irene's (Don's Mother) 48 Hour Salad 59
Carrot Rutabaga Bake 60
Pea and Peanut Slaw 61
Thousand Island Dressing (from the Lark Restaurant in Iowa City) 62
Crockpot Stuffing 63
Auntie Do Do's Ph'rench Dressing 64
Auntie Do Do's Blue Cheese Dressing 65
Make Ahead Potatoes 66
Hash Brown Au Gratin Casserole 67
Vegetable Strata Supreme 68
Zucchini Side Dish 69
Give 'n Take Chicken Salad 70

Soups, Stews & Eat-It-With-A-Fork Chowders

Cheddar Cheese Chowder 73
Hot Sour Soup 74
Hamburger Veggie Soup 76
Hearty Hash Brown Soup 77
Grand Casino Hinckley's Wild Rice Soup 78
Chicken Wild Rice Soup 79
New England Clam Chowder 80
White Bean and Pork Chili 82
Karen's Ph'amous Chili 83
Wisconsin Beer Cheese Soup 84
Chicken Tortilla Soup 85
Spicy Cheeseburger Soup 86
Veggie Cheese Soup 87
Chicken and Corn Chowder with Thyme 88
Beef Stew 89
White Chili 90
Auntie Do Do's Chili 91
Chili Bang-Bang 92

Breads, Sweet Rolls & Diet-Busting Muph'ins!

Pumpkin Bread 95
Sky High Popovers 96
Energy Muph'ins 97
Mom's Zucchini Bread 98
Maple Bar Muph'ins 99
Polish Coffee Cake 100

Banana Bread 101
Jewish Coffee Cake 102
Big Dog Sweet Rolls 103
Monkey Bread 104
Pepperoni Bread 105
Amaretto Cheese Danish 106
Cheesy Sourdough Bread 107
Ginger Cream Scones 108

Ph'rom Morning 'til Night Ph'abulous Main Events

Morning ...

Make-Ahead Breakfast Casserole 111
Aebleskiver (Danish Pancake Balls) 112
Cotter Band "Wake-Up" Egg Casserole 113
Grandpa Ted's Ph'rench Pancakes 114
Ph'rench Pancakes 115
Potato Pancakes 116
Overnight Baked Ph'rench Toast 117
Maple Ph'rench Toast Bake 118
Sunday Brunch Eggs 119
Potatoes Crust Quiche 120
Mom's Sausage Egg Bake 121
Puffy Omelet with Shrimp and Creamy Parmesan Sauce 122

... 'til Night

Pepper Steak 123
Grandma's Baked Chicken and Rice 124

Seafood Crepes ... 125
Taco Hot Dish ... 126
Hot Beef Sandwich ... 127
Big Bob's Smoked Chicken with White BBQ Sauce ... 128
Bolognese-Style Meat Ragu ... 130
Mediterranean Ph'lounder ... 132
Short-Cut Paella ... 133
Cuban Shrimp and Rice ... 134
Parmesan Chicken ... 135
Pizza Hotdish ... 136
Palpettos ... 137
Golden Mushroom Chops ... 138
Parmesan Chicken ... 139
Sweet Mongolian Chicken ... 140
Baked Almond Chicken ... 141
Beefy Hash Brown Pizza ... 142
Bob Evans Sausage Gravy and Biscuits ... 143
Quick Spaghetti Sauce ... 144
Pork Chops with Mushroom Gravy ... 145
Phil's Ph'amous Baby Back Ribs ... 146
Blackened Spice ... 147
Enchiladas de Pollo ... 148
Creamy Chicken Lasagna ... 150
Pork Roast with Cranberry Glaze ... 151
Roasted Mediterranean Chicken ... 152
Reuben Spread ... 153
Escalloped Ph'ish ... 154
Henrietta's Chow Mein ... 155
Spicy Chicken Legs ... 156
Tator Tot Hot Dish ... 157
Chicken Casserole ... 158

Grandma Joanie's Meatballs and Noodles 159
Mashed Potatoes and Hamburger Gravy 160
Summertime Salmon 161
Party Chicken 162
Queso Flameado (Ph'laming Cheese) 163
Chicken Asparagus Casserole 164
Korean Style Short Ribs 165
Chicken and Mushroom Wellington 166
Slow Cooked Sesame Chicken 167
Ph'ried Rice with Shrimp 168
Chicken Lasagna 169
Smothered Burritos 170
Auntie Do Do's Chicken Ala King 171
Auntie Do Do's Ham Buns 172
Auntie Do Do's Chow Mein (crock pot version) 173
Chow Mein Hot Dish 174
Apricot Dijon Chicken 175
Chow Mein Noodle Hot Dish 176
(Crockpot) Hamburger Casserole 177
Crazy Crust Pizza 178
Crisp Crab Cakes with Chardonnay Cream Sauce 179
Olive Garden Ph'ettuccine Alfredo 180
Chicken Tarragon En Croute 181
Crab-Stuffed Chicken Breasts 182
Savory Stuffed Pork Chops 183
Portabella Mushroom Sandwiches with Tahini Sauce 184
Meat Loaf Supreme 185
Pheasant in Mushroom-Cream Sauce 186
Asian Lettuce Wraps 187
Baked Ph'ish with Stuffing 188
Pan-Ph'ried Walleye Ph'illets 189
Pistachio-Crusted Chicken with Herbs & Cream Sauce 190

Sinful Desserts & "Sticky Ph'ingers" Sweets

Pumpkin Marble Cheesecake 193
Steamed Cranberry Pudding 194
Earthquake Cake 195
Caramel Cheesecake Squares 196
Cherry Pecan Dessert 197
Sensational Peppermint Pattie Brownies 198
Turtle Bars 199
Rhubarb Whip Cream Cake 200
Mint Cake 201
Syllabub 202
Quick Ph'ruit Cobbler 203
7 Layer Bars 204
Rice Krispies Treats 205
Rhubarb Goop 206
Blueberry Dream Dessert 207
Banana Split 208
Old-Fashioned White Cookies 209
Pumpkin Torte 210
Special "K" Bars 211
Chocolate Caramel Bars 212
Rhubarb Cake 213
Salted Nut Bars 214
Applesauce Cake 215
Angel Gingerbread 216
Chocolate Bar Pie 217
Apple Pie Cake 218
Butterfinger Candies 219
Auntie Do Do's Bananas Frosting 220

Peanut Butter and Graham Cracker Toffee 221
Bev's Very Best Chocolate Chip Cookies 222
Bev's Caramel-Cashew Bars 223
Oreo Truffles (Cookies & Cream Candy) 224
Julie's Sugar Roll Outs 225
Chocolate Brownies 226
Ph'rench Silk Pie 227
Peanut Butter Pie 228
Cake Mix Coconut Macaroons 229
Pineapple Cream Cheese Dessert 230
Apple Crisp 231
Easy, Creamy Orange Truffles 232
Chocolate Turtle Cheesecake 233
Peanut Butter Bars 234
Pineapple Casserole 235
Auntie Do Do's Raspberry Jell-O 236
Peanut Butter Swirls 237
Chocolate Bundt Cake 238
Ph'ruit Pizza 239
Chocolate Chip-Malted Milk Cookies 240

Beverages, Bits & Tasty Misfits

Bailey's Irish Cream 243
Phil's Perfect Bloody Mary Mix 244
Grandma Roppes Iced Tea 245
Punch 246
Party Punch 247
Blackberry Wine Cooler 248
Corn and Pepper Relish 249
Bev's Beef Jerky 250
Jerky (venison or beef) 251

Carmel Corn 252
Auntie Do Do's Cream Gravy for Lutefisk 253
Quick and Easy Homemade Jam 254

Recipes Ph'rom Ph'amous People & Places!

Tom Cruise's Spaghetti Carbonara 257
Barba Guian (Rissoles) - Appetizer 258
Marinated Steak ala Burt 259
Herb Crispies 260
Mom Unser's "Indy" Chili 261
Artichoke Salad 262
Broccoli Casserole 263
Seafood Casserole 264
Onions Rozelle (on the barbecue) 266
Baja California Chicken 267
Frank Sinatra's Sauce 268
Almond Delights 269
Robert Duvall's Mother's Crab Cakes 270
Macadamia, Chocolate Chip and
Peanut Butter Mini-Turnovers 271

The Photo Gallery 273

Give-A-Little, Get-A-Lot 283

So, what's with swapping "f" with "ph" –?!

To answer that question you'd have to know the Staige ph'amily and how much ph'un they make out of li'phe. Every gathering is a party, and every party is a pleasure.

However, for this particular project, here is the real explanation ...

Phil Staige was diagnosed with a Glioblastoma Multiforme Grade IV brain tumor in January of 2004. When the committee formed to organize a benefit on Phil's behalf, his sister, Janet, suggested that replacing the "F" in the words 'friends" and "family" with the "Ph" of Phil's name represented a small but significant act of solidarity — both visually and aurally — towards the cause. We are a union of ph'amily and ph'riends willing to ph'ight this disease with Phil by giving our love and support to him, and we refuse to let him stand alone.

The letter swapping became contagious, and has spread rampantly from benefit supporters and recipe contributors, to the text throughout this book. It just keeps going (and going) ... much like that (often annoying) big, pink, drum-beating Bunny.

This book would not be possible if it weren't for the absolute dedication of the Staige ph'amily and ph'riends to Phil and each other. And, thanks to the technology of email and the internet, the ability to spread the word, and compile this book of recipes took only a matter of days, instead of the weeks, or even months, that are typically associated with a book project like this. Without the instant-access technology, and the willingness of people to meet an extremely short deadline, you would not now be holding this book in your hands.

People continue to ask how they can help. If you're one of them, we've included a few suggestions at the back of this book on page 277. None of them take much time, money or effort on your part, but will make a significant difference to the ph'amily, as Phil continues the treatments to battle this disease.

Our sincere thanks for your contribution to the Phil Staige Benefit by purchasing this book.

Ph'riends of Phil Committee Members:

Ph'riends: Nick Edstrom, Bev Keiper, Steve Koch, Jane Palmer, Jim Palmer, Carol Saecker, Eric Saecker

Ph'amily: Earl Staige, Phyllis Staige, Pat Staige, John Staige, Rose Mary Staige, Allen Staige, Joanie Staige, Janet (Staige) Stanton

Karen, Katie, Phil & Charlotte

Appetizers, Dips & Ruin-Your-Appetite Starters

Ph'abulous Creamy Dip with Toasted Pecan

Contributed by Janet Stanton
(Phil's sister)

Ingredients:

- **16 oz. cream cheese**
- **1 cup sour cream**
- **1 cup chopped pecans**
- **4 Tbsp. chopped onion**
- **1 tsp. garlic powder**
- **2 small packages chopped beef**
- **Box of crackers**

Directions:

Preheat oven to 350 degrees.

Toast the pecans in a little butter (about a Tbsp. or so).

Mix all other ingredients in a bowl and then spread in a pie pan.

Sprinkle pecans on top.

Bake for 20 minutes, serve warm on crackers.

Bacon-Ph'illed Cherry Tomatoes

Contributed by Jane Palmer

Ingredients:

- **1 lb. bacon, crisply cooked and crumbled**
- **¼ cup finely chopped green onions**
- **2 Tbsp. fresh parsley**
- **2 Tbsp. grated Parmesan cheese**
- **½ cup mayonnaise**
- **1 lb. cherry tomatoes**

Directions:

In medium bowl, combine bacon, onions, parsley, cheese and mayonnaise. Stir until well blended.

Remove stems from tomatoes. Place tomatoes, stem side down, on cutting board. Cut thin slices off of each.

With small spoon or melon scoop, carefully hollow out tomato, leaving ½ inch thick shell. Invert tomatoes on paper towels and drain.

Fill tomatoes with bacon mixture. Garnish as desired.

Refrigerate overnight or several hours to blend flavors.

Do Ahead Cheese Puffs

Contributed by Inez Miller
(Ph'riend of a ph'riend)

Ingredients:

- **2 cups shredded sharp process cheese - 8 oz.**
- **1/2 cup butter or margarine softened**
- **1 cup all-purpose flour**
- **1 tsp. freeze dried chives**
- **1/2 tsp. seasoned salt**

Directions:

Mix cheese and butter; stir in flour, chives, and seasoned salt until blended.

Shape into 1 inch balls.

Place on ungreased baking sheet, cover and refrigerate up to 48 hours.

Bake at 400 degrees until light brown. Let set 15 minutes before serving.

Cook's Tip!

If chunk cheese becomes too dry, place it in a shallow dish with a 1-inch layer of buttermilk, cover and refrigerate overnight.

Jack Daniels Honey Mustard Glazed Ribs

Contributed by Walt Miller
(Ph'riend of a ph'riend)

Marinade Ingredients:

- **1/2 cup Jack Daniels**
- **1/2 cup red cooking wine**
- **3/4 cup chopped onion**
- **6 cloves of garlic minced**
- **1 cup honey**
- **1/2 cup ketchup**
- **4 Tbsp. worcestershire sauce**
- **1 tsp. tobasco**
- **2 Tbsp. dry hot Chinese mustard**
- **1 tsp. cumin**
- **1 tsp. minced ginger**

Pork short ribs

Directions:

Combine marinade and cook until reduced and thickened.

Marinate ribs in sauce overnight.

Grill ribs and baste with marinade.

Reserve sauce and warm for dipping.

Baked Potato Chips

Contributed by Susan Carter

Ingredients:

- **Baking potatoes**
- **Vegetable cooking spray**
- **Sea salt**

Directions:

Cut potatoes in half crosswise, exposing two flat surfaces.

Use a vegetable peeler to cut paper-thin slices. Spray them lightly with vegetable oil and arrange in a single layer on a baking sheet.

Bake at 450 degrees for about 10-12 minutes or until lightly golden brown.

Place chips in a paper bag with a small amount of sea salt (1/4 tsp. per potato) and shake to season.

Cook's Tip!

Need a quick dip? Whir cottage cheese in your blender and add herbs or onion soup mix to taste.

Chicken Wings

Contributed by Jane Palmer

Ingredients:

- **4 lbs. chicken wings**
- **½ cup soy sauce**
- **½ cup brown sugar**
- **½ cup butter**
- **¼ cup water**
- **½ tsp. dry mustard**

Directions:

Mix together all ingredients (except chicken wings) and cook 5 minutes.

Cool and brush over wings.

Bake at 350 degrees for 1 hour, turning and basting often.

Pesto Shrimp Pizza Bites

Contributed by Susan Carter

Ingredients:

- **2 small (6-inch) Boboli Italian pizza crusts**
- **1/2 cup prepared pesto sauce**
- **1 bunch green onions, diced**
- **1/2 lb. cooked shrimp**
- **3/4 cup Cojack or combination of mozzarella and cheddar cheese, shredded**
- **1/3 cup shredded parmesan or asiago cheese**

Directions:

Spread 1/4 cup pesto onto each crust.
Top each with green onions, shrimp and cheese.

Bake in 350 degree oven approximately 15 minutes until cheese melts. Broil for the last 2 minutes, if desired.

Crab Stuffed Mushrooms

Contributed by Jane Palmer

Ingredients:

- **20 large mushroom caps**
- **Kraft Italian dressing**
- **1 ½ cups flaked crabmeat**
- **¾ cup fresh bread crumbs**
- **2 eggs, beaten**
- **¼ cup mayonnaise**
- **¼ cup minced onion**
- **1 tsp. lemon juice**

Directions:

Marinate mushrooms in Italian dressing; drain.

Combine crabmeat, ½ cup crumbs, eggs, mayonnaise, onion and lemon juice; fill mushrooms.

Top with remaining crumbs.

Bake at 375 degrees for 15 minutes.

Cook's Tip!

If you need only half an onion, use the top half and refrigerate the root bottom. It will store longer in the fridge.

Wonton Appetizers

Contributed by Jody Boughton
(Phil's cousin)

Ingredients:

- **2 lbs. Jimmy Dean sausage, browned**
- **1 pkg. Hidden Valley Ranch dressing, prepared as directed on package**
- **1 ½ cups Monterey Jack cheese, shredded**
- **1 ½ cups sharp cheddar, shredded**
- **1 small can black olives, sliced**
- **Wonton skins**

Directions:

Combine sausage, dressing, cheeses and olives. Spray cupcake tines with vegetable cooking spray. Place ½ wonton skin in each tin and spray again. Bake 5 minutes in 400 degree oven (store won ton skins in storage bag until ready to use). Place baked skins on a cookie sheet and fill with mixture. Bake at 400 degrees until cheese is melted.

A party hit!

Wonton Dipping Chips

Contributed by Susan Carter

Ingredients:

- **6 Tbsp. butter, melted**
- **20 wonton skins**
- **Course salt or Italian seasoning**

Directions:

Preheat oven to 375 degrees.

Brush a baking sheet with some of the melted butter.

Cut wonton skins into shapes of your choice using cookie cutters, or simply cut skins diagonally with sharp knife to form triangles.

Place as many pieces as you can fit onto the baking sheet – skins do not spread during baking.

Brush tops with butter and sprinkle with course salt or Italian seasoning.

Bake for approximately 5 minutes or until crisp but not too brown. Cool.

Serve with your favorite dips.

Taco Dip

Contributed by Lynn Johnson & "Big Jer"
(Phil's cousin)

Ingredients:

- **1 large cream cheese**
- **1 carton sour cream**
- **1 Tbsp. seasoned salt (Lowrys)**
- **1 ripe avocado (soft)**
- **1 onion, chopped**
- **1 head lettuce, shredded**
- **Shredded cheese**
- **Tomato, chopped**
- **Black olives, optional**

Directions:

Blend cream cheese, sour cream, seasoned salt and avacado. Spread on platter.

Top with remaining ingredients.

Cook's Tip! Make your own sour cream by combining 1 Tbsp. lemon juice with evaporated whole milk to make one cup. Let stand at room temperature for about 40 minutes.

Hot Artichoke Dip and Crackers

Contributed by Jane Palmer

Ingredients:

- **14 oz. can artichoke hearts (in water)**
- **1 cup Parmesan cheese**
- **1 cup shredded mozzarella or cheddar cheese**
- **¾ cup mayonnaise**
- **½ tsp. garlic powder**
- **2 Tbsp. chopped onion**
- **2 Tbsp. chopped parsley**

Directions:

Drain and chop artichokes. Add remaining ingredients.

Grease an 8x8 inch Pyrex dish.

Transfer mixture to dish and bake at 350 degrees for 25 to 30 minutes. Check the last few minutes to avoid over baking.

Serve warm with an assortment of crackers.

Salads, Slaws & I-Want-A-Second-Helping Side Dishes

Curried Chicken Salad

Contributed by Sara Schmanski

Mix together:

- **3 Tbsp. instant onion**
- **3 Tbsp. water**

Let stand for 10 minutes.

Sauté for 3 to 5 minutes:

- **2 Tbsp. butter**
- **1 ¼ tsp. curry powder**
- **the instant onion mixture from above**

Add the curry mixture to:

- **1/3 cup mayonnaise**
- **1 Tbsp. lemon juice**
- **½ tsp. salt**
- **dash of cayenne pepper**

Mix together:

- **3 cups diced cooked chicken**
- **1 large can pineapple chunks**
- **½ cup coarsely chopped nuts (I use walnuts)**
- **1/3 cup golden raisins**
- **1 red apple diced (I use Fuji)**
- **2 Tbsp. shredded coconut**

Blend chicken mixture with dressing and enjoy.

Orange Fluff

Contributed by Linda Grupa

Ingredients:

- **1 3-ounce box orange Jell-O**
- **1 small vanilla pudding (cooking kind, not instant)**
- **1 small tapioca pudding (cooking kind, not instant)**
- **1 large can mandarin oranges**
- **8 ounces Cool Whip**
- **3 cups hot water**

Directions:

Mix puddings and Jell-O with hot water.

Cook on low heat until thickened.

Cool - usually a few hours.

Add cool whip and mandarin oranges. Mix thoroughly and chill until serving time.

Cook's Tip!

For a quick and tasty fruit dressing, grate the zest from an orange and mix with orange juice and sour cream.

Mushroom Corn Casserole

Contributed by Jim Grupa

Ingredients:

- **1/3 cup chopped green pepper**
- **1/3 cup finely chopped onion**
- **3 Tbls. butter or margarine, divided**
- **1/4 cup all-purpose flour**
- **1 can (14-3/4 ounces) cream-style corn**
- **1/2 tsp. salt**
- **1/8 tsp. pepper**
- **1 pkg. (3 ounces) cream cheese, cubed**
- **1 can (15-1/4 ounces) whole kernel corn, drained**
- **1 can (4 ounces) mushroom stems and pieces, drained**
- **1/2 cup shredded Swiss cheese**
- **1-1/2 cups bread crumbs**

Directions:

In a sauce pan, saute green pepper and onion in 1 tablespoon butter until tender.

Stir in flour, cream corn, salt and pepper until blended.

Add cream cheese; stir until melted.

Stir in the whole kernel corn, mushrooms and Swiss cheese.

Transfer to a greased 1-1/2 quart baking dish.

Melt remaining butter; toss with bread crumbs. Sprinkle over the corn mixture.

Bake, uncovered, at 400 degrees F. for 20-25 minutes or until heated through.

Grandma's 24 Hour Salad

Contributed by Carol Saecker

Ingredients:

- **3 egg yolks**
- **2 Tbsp. sugar**
- **Dash of salt**
- **2 Tbsp. vinegar**
- **1 Tbsp. butter**
- **1 cup heavy cream, whipped**
- **2 cups pineapple bits in syrup – reserve 2 Tbsp. of syrup**
- **2 cups pitted white cherries, drained**
- **2 cups quartered marshmallows**
- **2 oranges, cut in pieces**

Directions:

Cook egg yolks, sugar, salt, vinegar, pineapple syrup and butter in double boiler, until thick. Cool.

Fold in whipped cream, pineapple bits, white cherries, marshmallows and orange pieces. Chill 24 hours.

Decorate top with additional orange slices and maraschino cherries, if desired.

Barbecued Bean Salad

This salad is great for buffets, serves as an all-vegetarian dish and makes a great side dish for any barbecued meat or poultry.

Contributed by Sara Schmanski

Ingredients:

- **1 (16 oz.) pkg. pinto beans**
- **1/3 cup each ketchup and cider vinegar**
- **¼ cup olive oil**
- **1 ½ Tbsp. worcestershire sauce**
- **¼ cup brown sugar, packed**
- **1 ½ Tbsp. chili powder**
- **1 ½ tsp. ground cumin**
- **1 tsp. salt**
- **¼ tsp. pepper**
- **¼ tsp. red-pepper sauce**
- **2 Tbsp. Dijon mustard**
- **1 each, medium red and green bell pepper, diced**
- **1 medium white or sweet onion, minced**
- **1 11-ounce can kernel corn, drained**
- **6 ounces plain corn tortilla chips, crumbled (divided)**

Directions:

Rinse, soak over night, and cook beans according to package directions until tender but not falling apart, about 45 minutes. Drain, rinse under cold running water and drain well again.

In a small non aluminum saucepan, combine ketchup, vinegar, oil, Worcestershire, sugar, chili powder, cumin, salt, pepper and pepper sauce. Bring to a boil, lower heat and simmer 10 minutes. Remove from heat and whisk in mustard and set aside.

In a large bowl combine cooked beans, bell peppers, onion, corn and cooled dressing. Just before serving fold in half of the crumbled chips into the salad. Sprinkle remaining chips over top. Serve at room temperature. Can be made the day before.

Marketplace Salad

Contributed by Sharon Woychek

Ingredients:

- **1 head torn romaine**
- **1/2 bunch sliced green onions**
- **2 stalks diced celery**
- **1 cup sliced water chestnuts**
- **1 diced red pepper**
- **1/2 cup slivered toasted almonds**
- **1 cup diced cooked chicken**
- **Mandarin oranges for garnish**

Directions:

Mix all together with bottled or homemade poppyseed dressing.

Chinese Noodle Salad

Contributed by Inez Miller
(Ph'riend of a ph'riend)

Salad Ingredients:

- **1/2 cup butter**
- **Large pkg. slivered almonds**
- **1/3 cup sesame seeds**
- **Pkg. Ramen noodles crushed**
- **1 head of bok choy, chopped**
- **Green onions, chopped (2 bunches)**

In skillet, melt butter, and lightly saute almonds, sesame seeds and noodles.

Toss with bok choy and green onions.

Dressing ingredients:

- **1 cup oil (could be combination of olive and regular oil)**
- **2 Tbsp. soy sauce**
- **1 cup sugar**
- **1/2 cup Tarragon vinegar**
- **Contents of Ramen seasoning packet**

Blend all ingredients in mixer.

Assemble only as much as needed as it won't keep.

Seasoned Unfried Ph'rench Ph'ries

Contributed by Susan Carter

Ingredients:

- **5 large baking potatoes, washed and dried**
- **Vegetable oil or vegetable oil cooking spray**
- **2 large egg whites, fork-whipped**
- **1 Tbsp. cajun spice**

Directions:

Move oven rack to bottom position, and preheat oven to 400 degrees.

Slice each potato lengthwise into 1/4 inch ovals, and then slice each oval lengthwise into 1/4 inch matchsticks.

Liberally coat a baking sheet with vegetable oil.

Combine the egg whites and Cajun spice in a large bowl. Add the matchstick potatoes and mix to coat.

Pour the coated potatoes onto the prepared baking sheet and spread them into a single layer.

Bake for 40-45 minutes, turning every 7-8 minutes, until the fries are crispy and evenly browned.

Serve immediately.

Pasta Salad

Note: This salad I make for large gatherings. It is quite a bit of work but is worth it. Keeps well in the refrigerator for a few days. You can use cotto salami, but I like the hard Genoa salami cut in fourths. This recipe serves about 20-25 people.

Contributed by Helen Sheldon
(Phil's aunt)

Ingredients:

- **1 16 oz. pkg. of rotini pasta**
- **1 good-sized cucumber, peeled and cubed**
- **1 can pitted black olives (sliced)**
- **1 small jar stuffed green olives, sliced**
- **1 cup celery, chopped**
- **1 large green pepper, chopped**
- **I/2 of a large red pepper, chopped**
- **2 large carrots, shredded**
- **1 bunch fresh broccoli, use the flowerettes**
- **1 red onion, sliced very fine**
- **12 cherry tomatoes, cut in half or quarters**
- **1 tsp. Italian seasoning**
- **3 cups mozzarella cheese, grated**
- **1/2 lb. Genoa salami, cut in half or quarters**
- **1 large bottle of Zesty Italian dressing or Paul Newman's Family Style Italian**

Directions:

Toss all together in a very large bowl. Make one day ahead to blend flavors. Keeps well in refrigerator. You can use two different pastas if you desire. Cook pasta according to directions.

Serves at least 25 people.

Calico Beans

Contributed by Helen Sheldon
(Phil's aunt)

Ingredients:

- **1 lb. good ground beef**
- **1 lb. good brand of bacon**
- **2 large onions chopped**
- **1/4 cup granulated sugar**
- **2/3 cup packed brown sugar**
- **1/2 cup ketchup**
- **1/2 cup barbecue sauce**
- **1/4 cup prepared mustard**
- **1/4 cup molasses**
- **1 tsp. chili powder**
- **2 tsp. salt (scant)**
- **1 tsp. pepper**
- **2 cans red kidney beans**
- **2 cans lima beans**
- **2 28 oz. cans pork and beans (I use Bushes)**

Directions:

Dice bacon and saute until crisp.

Add the ground beef and chopped onion and cook until meat loses all red color. Carefully drain off all the fat.

Mix together the sugars, ketchup, barbecue sauce, mustard, molasses, chili powder, salt and pepper. Add to first mixture along with the cans of undrained beans. Place in roaster.

Cover and bake in moderate oven (350 degrees) for one and one-half hours. Uncover the last half hour of baking if mixture is too juicy. Freezes very well.

Calico Beans

And, for a slightly different version ...

Contributed by Janet Stanton
(Phil's sister)

Ingredients:

- **1/2 lb. hamburger**
- **1/2 lb. bacon**
- **1 cup chopped onions**
- **1/2 cup ketchup**
- **1 tsp. mustard**
- **3/4 cup brown sugar**
- **2 tsp. vinegar**
- **1 pound can each of:**
  kidney beans (drained)
  lima beans (drained)
  pork & beans with tomato sauce

Directions:

Brown hamburger and onion.

Cook bacon then break it up.

Mix remaining ingredients well.

Add beans and meat.

Bake 1 hour at 350 degrees.

Freezes well.

Super Pasta and Vegetable Salad

Contributed by Linda Bethke

Ingredients:

- **1 lb. mostaccioli noodles or other pasta**
- **2 Tbsp. chicken soup mix**
- **1 to 2 cucumbers diced**
- **1 large tomato diced**
- **1 small onion finely diced**
- **1 green pepper finely diced**

Sweet Herb Dressing:

- **1 ½ cups salad oil**
- **1 cup vinegar**
- **½ cup of sugar**
- **1 Tbsp. parsley**
- **2 tsp. French or German mustard**
- **2 tsp. dried minced onion**
- **1 tsp. garlic powder granules**
- **¾ tsp. black pepper**
- **½ tsp. celery seed**
- **Chicken soup mix**

Directions:

Cook mostaccioli according to package directions, except substitute chicken soup mix for salt, drain and cool.

Add cucumbers, tomato, onion, and green pepper.

Pour enough sweet herb dressing over salad to moisten. Refrigerate several hours.

Makes 5 quarts.

Artichoke Rice Salad

Contributed by Sara Schmanski

Ingredients:

- **1 pkg. of Chicken Rice-a-Roni**
- **2 green onions, chopped**
- **½ green pepper, chopped**
- **2 jars of marinated artichoke hearts, cut up**
- **6 stuffed olives, sliced**
- **¼ tsp. curry powder**
- **1/3 cup mayonnaise**
- **Salt and pepper to taste**

Directions:

Cook Rice-a-Roni as directed on package. Cool.

Add remaining ingredients.

Chill before serving.

If desired, add mushrooms and shrimp. I only use 1 jar of the artichokes and a little of the juice.

Bev's Pasta Salad

Contributed by Bev Keiper

Ingredients:

- **1 lb. cooked linguine, chilled**
- **8 oz. Zesty Italian salad dressing**
- **4 Tbsp. Salad Supreme seasoning**
- **Pepperoni**
- **Assorted chopped vegetables such as red & green peppers, green olives, broccoli, etc.**

Directions:

Combine cooked linguine with Zesty Italian Salad dressing and "Salad Supreme" seasoning.

Add pepperoni to taste (microwave pepperoni before putting in salad).

Toss with an assortment of chopped vegetables.

Serve cold.

Joyce Farrell's Ph'ruit Salad Dressing

Contributed by Sara Schmanski

Ingredients:

- **1 3-ounce package of vanilla instant pudding**
- **1 15 ¼ oz. can crushed pineapple ... do not drain**
- **1 pint sour cream**
- **2 ½ Tbsp. fresh lemon juice**

Directions:

Mix together all ingredients and toss with your favorite fruits to make a great salad.

This will store in refrigerator for up to 2 weeks.

Pico de Gallo

An authentic Mexican salad from Oaxaca, Mexico.

Contributed by Dale C. Howe
(Ph'riend of a ph'riend)

Ingredients:

- **2 cups chopped red tomato**
- **2 cups chopped green bell pepper**
- **2 cups chopped white onion**
- **1 cup chopped cilantro**
- **2 cloves minced garlic**
- **2 minced serano peppers (include seeds)**
- **1 tsp. cumin**
- **2 Tbsp. salt**
- **Juice from a fresh lime**

Directions:

Mix all ingredients in a plastic, glass or ceramic bowl. Cover and chill in the refrigerator for 3 hours before serving. Great as a side dish or on tacos.

NOTE: The serano peppers make this salad "hot" — but you can tame it by substituting jalapeno peppers that have had the seeds and membrane removed.

Cook's Tip!

To ripen tomatoes, place them stem side down in a cool place, spaced so that they are not touching.

Billie's Spinach Salad

This is Dons favorite recipe in the whole world. I think he would even have it for breakfast if I would serve it. Thank God for Billie Jueneaux, my dear friend and bridge partner at Eagle Lake, for she shared this recipe several years ago.

Contributed by Sara Schmanski

Ingredients:

- **2 bunches spinach**
- **2 pkgs. Top Ramen, no seasoning**
- **1 pkg. slivered almonds**
- **½ ounce sesame seeds**
- **½ cube butter**
- **1 bunch of green onions, sliced**
- **Prepared dressing (below)**

Directions:

Crush noodles in a bag and brown in butter with seed and almonds. Mix with spinach and onions.

Toss with following dressing:

- ½ cup oil
- ¼ cup cider vinegar
- ¼ cup sugar
- 2 Tbsp. soy sauce

Shake in a jar.

Hash Brown Cheese Potatoes

Contributed by Jane Palmer

Ingredients:

- **2-lb pkg. frozen shredded hash browns**
- **16 oz. sour cream**
- **10 ¾ oz can Cream of Chicken soup**
- **1 small onion chopped**
- **8 ounces (2 cups) shredded cheddar cheese**
- **Potato chips**
- **½ cup butter, melted**

Directions:

Thaw hash browns 1 hour.

Heat oven to 350 degrees.

In large bowl, mix sour cream and soup. Stir in hash browns, onion and cheese. Spoon into ungreased 9 x 12 x 2 inch pan.

Crush potato chips in bag with rolling pin. Sprinkle top of casserole with potato chips.

Pour melted butter over all.

Bake for 1 hour.

Copper Penny's

Another great salad recipe from the "salad queen" Billy Juneaux. This sweet sour dish is a great Thanksgiving side dish and you can make ahead and freeze.

Contributed by Sara Schmanski

Ingredients:

- **2 lbs. carrots**
- **1 green pepper**
- **1 medium onion**
- **1 10-ounce can of tomato soup**
- **½ cup olive oil**
- **½ cup vinegar**
- **2/3 cup sugar**
- **1 Tbsp. mustard**

Directions:

Slice carrots and cook in water until half done, drain.

Mix all remaining ingredients with carrots and continue cooking until done.

Jo Shipleys Cucumbers

I played Bridge with Jo in Carson City and she was a great source of fabulous recipes...this is one of my favorites.

Contributed by Sara Schmanski

Ingredients:

- **4 cucumbers sliced thin (I use food processor)**
- **1/3 cup white vinegar**
- **¼ cup sugar**
- **¼ tsp. pepper**
- **2 Tbsp. chopped parsley**

Directions:

Layer cucumbers in a bowl and salt each layer. Put a weight on top and refrigerate overnight.

Next day squeeze out water and rinse.

Mix the remaining ingredients and pour over the cucumbers.

Billy's Poppy Lime Dressing

This is a great salad recipe from Billy, and loved by my dinner guests.

Contributed by Sara Schmanski

Dressing Ingredients:

- **1/3 cup apple cider vinegar**
- **1/3 cup lime juice**
- **¾ cup sugar**
- **1 tsp. salt**
- **1 tsp. dry mustard**
- **1 tsp. paprika**
- **1 cup olive oil**
- **1 tsp. onion juice**
- **1 tsp. poppy seed**

Blend all in blender till thickened. Refrigerate.

Salad ingredients:

- **Mixed greens**
- **Grapefruit sections**
- **Red onions (slices)**
- **Avocado (slices)**

Cook's Tip!

A small amount of salt will make a grapefruit taste sweeter.

Poppy Seed Dressing for Ph'ruit

Contributed by Sara Schmanski

Ingredients:

- **1 ½ cup sugar**
- **2 tsp. dry mustard**
- **2 tsp. salt**
- **2/3 cup vinegar**
- **3 Tbsp. onion juice**
- **2 cups olive oil**

Directions:

Mix in blender and then add:

- **3 Tbsp. poppy seed**

Leaf Lettuce with Buttermilk Dressing

Contributed by Sara Schmanski

Ingredients:

- **¼ cup buttermilk**
- **2 Tbsp. mayonnaise**
- **2 Tbsp. sugar**
- **1 Tbsp. vinegar**
- **6 cups torn leaf lettuce**

Directions:

In a small bowl, whisk the first four ingredients.

Toss with lettuce or serve on the side.

Cook's Tip!

Snip the tops of carrots into salads - they are high in vitamins K and E that aren't in the carrot itself!

Exotic Chicken Salad

*I got this recipe from Addie Stebbin of Eagle Lake.
On the recipe card I had filed in my box I had put four stars
and also note that the recipe was excellent!*

Contributed by Sara Schmanski

Ingredients:

- **4 cups cooked chicken, cut in bite-sized cubes**
- **2 7-oz. cans water chestnuts, sliced**
- **2 cans pineapple chunks, drained**
- **2 cups celery, finely sliced**
- **1 ½ cups mayonnaise**
- **1 ½ Tbsp. honey**
- **2 Tbsp. soy sauce**
- **2 Tbsp. lemon juice**
- **1 Tbsp. curry powder**
- **½ tsp. salt**

Directions:

Prepare and lightly mix together the chicken, water chestnuts, pineapple and celery.

Mix remaining ingredients to make dressing and combine with first mixture.

Serve on red lettuce and garnish with slices of peeled cantaloupe, fresh strawberries and sliced almonds.

Cherry Pie Ph'illing Salad

Contributed by Jean Baker

Ingredients:

- **1 large Cool Whip**
- **15 oz. can crushed pineapple, drained**
- **1/4 cup lemon juice**
- **1 can cherry pie filling**
- **1 can sweetened condensed milk**

Directions:

Mix Cool Whip and milk.

Add pineapple, then cherry pie filling. Mix.

Add lemon juice and mix well.

Refrigerate.

This salad may be made the night before. Makes a good sized salad.

Cook's Tip!

Berry juice stains can usually be removed from your hands with lemon juice.

Our Ph'amily's Ph'avorite Cole Slaw

Contributed by Sara Schmanski

Slaw Ingredients:

- **1 large whole cabbage, finely chopped**
- **3 green onions, finely chopped**
- **1 green pepper, finely chopped**

Dressing Ingredients:

- **½ cup mayonnaise**
- **½ cup sour cream**
- **3 to 4 Tbsp. red vinegar**
- **1 tsp. salt**
- **¼ tsp. pepper**
- **¼ cup sugar**

May be prepared a day or 2 ahead of time.

Chinese Chicken Salad

Contributed by Sara Schmanski

Ingredients:

- **4 chicken breast, broiled or boiled, and shredded.**

Dressing:

- **½ cup white vinegar**
- **6 Tbsp. olive oil**
- **2 tsp. ginger**
- **4 Tbsp. soy sauce**
- **1 cup sugar**

For the salad:

- **2 heads of iceberg lettuce**
- **4 Tbsp. sesame seeds toasted**
- **1 cup cashews**
- **6 oz. chow mein noodles**

'Hold-the-Eggs & Anchovies' Caesar Salad

Contributed by Susan Carter

Ingredients:

- **1 head Romaine lettuce, cleaned & torn**
- **¼ cup extra-virgin olive oil, or enough to lightly coat lettuce**
- **1-2 Tbsp. fresh or bottled lemon juice**
- **1 Tbsp. fresh minced garlic**
- **2/3 cup grated Parmesan cheese**
- **Herbed or Caesar salad croutons (optional)**

Directions:

Put lettuce in salad bowl, pour olive oil and lemon juice over greens and toss. Sprinkle with minced garlic and parmesan; toss. Top with croutons and serve with additional grated cheese on the side.

This is also great topped with mesquite-grilled chicken cutlets or large cooked shrimp.

Cook's Tip!

To make a creamy salad dressing without cream, put all ingredients - except the oil - into a blender and turn it on. Very slowly, pour in cold-pressed olive oil.

Irene's (Don's Mother) 48 Hour Salad

Contributed by Sara Schmanski

Ingredients:

- **1 3-ounce package lemon Jell-O**
- **Small can crushed pineapple**
- **1 egg, beaten**
- **1/4 cup milk**
- **1 lemon**
- **1 cup whipping cream**
- **1/2 lb. miniature marshmallows**
- **1/2 cup slivered almonds**

Directions:

Dissolve Jell-O in 1 cup boiling water.

Drain pineapple and use juice with enough water to make 1 cup. Add to the Jell-O. Refrigerate.

Cook the egg, milk and lemon (both juice and zest of the rind) in a double boiler for 10 minutes. Cool.

Whip the whipping cream.

Fold all of the above together with the marshmallows, almonds, and the crushed pineapple.

Set in the refrigerator to gel and stir a couple of times the first hour.

Carrot Rutabaga Bake

This is an original that I make every Thanksgiving and it all goes!

Contributed by Ruth Holdorf
(Ph'amily of a ph'riend)

Ingredients:

- **2 lb. bag of carrots**
- **1 large or 2 small rutabaga**
- **1/4 cup packed brown sugar**
- **1 cup half and half**
- **2 beaten eggs**

Directions:

Clean and cook until tender both the carrots and the rutabaga. (I cook them separately.) Mash both of them and combine them in a big bowl.

Add the remaining ingredients and stir to incorporate completely.

Put in a 9x13 inch pan and bake in a 350 degree oven for 45 minutes to one hour or until set.

Serve hot.

You can mix everything the day before and refrigerate until one hour before dinner.

Pea and Peanut Slaw

Contributed by Sara Schmanski

Ingredients:

- **1 10-oz package frozen peas**
- **2 cups shredded cabbage**
- **1 green onion, sliced**

Dressing:

- **½ cup sour cream**
- **¼ cup mayo**
- **¼ tsp. salt**
- **¼ tsp. curry powder**
- **¼ tsp. pepper**
- **1 tsp. prepared mustard**
- **1 tsp. red wine vinegar**

3/4 cup Spanish peanuts

Directions:

Toss together peas, cabbage and green onion.

Mix together dressing ingredients and pour over greens. Toss.

Add ¾ cup Spanish peanuts just before serving.

Thousand Island Dressing (from the Lark Restaurant in Iowa City)

Contributed by Kathy Sheridan
(Ph'riend of a ph'riend)

Ingredients:

- **1 pint mayonnaise**
- **1 Tbsp. onion juice**
- **1/2 cup chopped green olives**
- **1 Tbsp. horseradish**
- **2 chopped hard boiled eggs**
- **2 dill pickles, grated**
- **1 Tbsp. worcestershire sauce**
- **1/3 bottle chili sauce**

Directions:

Blend all ingredients together. Use with your favorite salad ingredients.

Makes one quart and lasts two weeks. You'll never go back to off-the-shelf dressing again!

Cook's Tip!

You can prevent boiled eggs from cracking by rubbing a cut lemon on the shells before cooking.

Crockpot Stuffing

Contributed by Jody Boughton
(Phil's cousin)

Ingredients:

- **2 cups chicken broth**
- **½ cup onion, chopped**
- **½ cup celery, chopped**
- **8 cups bread crumbs**
- **½ cup butter**
- **1 tsp. salt**
- **1 ½ tsp. poultry seasoning**
- **¼ tsp. pepper**

Directions:

Melt butter and sauté onions and celery. Add seasonings and combine remaining ingredients. Put in crockpot and cover; cook on high for 1 hour, then set on low for ½ hour.

Auntie Do Do's Ph'rench Dressing

Contributed by Lynn Johnson & "Big Jer"
(Phil's cousin)

Ingredients:

- **1 cup oil**
- **½ cup sugar**
- **1 cup ketchup**
- **3 Tbsp. vinegar**
- **½ tsp. salt**
- **1 tsp. grated onion**
- **1 tsp. celery seed**

Directions:

Blend oil and sugar in blender, approximately 4 minutes.

Add remaining ingredients.

If you'd like, you can crumble some blue cheese into this recipe.

Auntie Do Do's Blue Cheese Dressing

Contributed by Lynn Johnson & "Big Jer"
(Phil's cousin)

Ingredients:

- **1 egg**
- **¾ tsp. salt**
- **½ tsp. dry mustard**
- **¼ tsp. paprika**
- **1 Tbsp. vinegar**
- **1 Tbsp. lemon juice**
- **1 cup oil**
- **8 ounces sour cream**
- **4 ounces blue cheese**
- **Dash of garlic salt**

Directions:

Blend first six ingredients together to make mayonnaise. Slowly add oil, ¼ cup at a time. Add sour cream and garlic salt. Pour out of blender and crumble in blue cheese.

Make Ahead Potatoes

Contributed by Lynn Johnson & "Big Jer"
(Phil's cousin)

Ingredients:

- **5 lbs. cooked, mashed potatoes**
- **8 ounces cream cheese**
- **1 cup half-and-half**
- **1 stick of butter**

Directions:

Mix all ingredients together, sprinkle with paprika, and bake at 350 degrees for 45 minutes.

Hash Brown Au Gratin Casserole

Contributed by Lynn Johnson & "Big Jer"
(Phil's cousin)

Ingredients:

- **2 lbs. hash browns, frozen, Southern style**
- **¼ lb. margarine, cut up**
- **1 pt. whipping cream**
- **2 cups shredded Swiss cheese**
- **Salt and pepper to taste**

Directions:

In a buttered 9x13 inch pan, layer ingredients in the order listed. Top with paprika.

Bake in 375 degree oven, uncovered, for one hour.

Cook's Tip!

When grating cheese, spray vegetable oil or nonstick cooking spray on the grater to make cleanup easier.

Vegetable Strata Supreme

Contributed by Jody Boughton
(Phil's cousin)

Ingredients:

- **6 slices white or wheat bread**
- **1 cup cooked ham, chopped**
- **8 eggs or egg substitute**
- **1 ½ cups milk**
- **1 tsp. dry mustard**
- **1 tsp. onion powder**
- **16 ounce package frozen broccoli, cauliflower and carrot combination**
- **1 ½ cups (6 ounces) shredded cheddar cheese**

Directions:

Grease 9x13 inch pan. Cut bread into ½ inch cubes. In medium bowl beat together eggs, milk, dry mustard and onion powder. Arrange vegetables in bottom of dish. Sprinkle vegetables with bread crumbs and ham. Pour egg mixture over all. Sprinkle with cheese. Cover with plastic wrap and refrigerate overnight.

Bake, uncovered, in preheated 350 degree oven for 40-50 minutes or until knife inserted near center comes out clean.

Zucchini Side Dish

Contributed by Jody Boughton
(Phil's cousin)

Ingredients:

- **1 large onion, chopped**
- **½ cup vegetable oil**
- **½ cup grated parmesan**
- **4 eggs, beaten**
- **1 Tbsp. fresh parsley**
- **3 cups grated zucchini**
- **1 cup Bisquick**
- **1 cup shredded cheddar cheese**

Directions:

Combine first 5 ingredients. Stir in zucchini, Bisquick and cheese. Pour into greased 9 x 13 inch pan. Bake 35 minutes at 350 degrees.

For half recipe, use a pie plate.

Give 'n Take Chicken Salad

Contributed by Susan Carter

Ingredients:

1 5-ounce chicken breast, roasted and shredded

Salad Mix:
- **1 lb. napa cabbage, shredded**
- **1/2 lb. shredded red cabbage**
- **1/4 cup shredded carrot**
- **1/4 cup bean sprouts**
- **8 wonton skins, cut into strips and quick fried in hot oil until golden brown; drain on paper towel**
- **1/4 cup scallions, julienned**

Dressing:
- **1/2 cup soy sauce**
- **1/2 cup rice vinegar (or white wine vinegar)**
- **2 Tbsp. white sugar**
- **2 Tbsp. ginger, finely chopped**
- **1/4 cup yellow onion, peeled, finely diced**
- **1/4 cup canola oil**
- **2 Tbsp. scallions, julienned**

Nut topping:
- **1 cup walnuts, rough chopped**
- **1 Tbsp. unsalted butter, room temperature**
- **1 Tbsp. chili pepper flakes**
- **1 Tbsp. honey**

Directions:

Combine all the salad mix ingredients together, toss well. In a separate bowl, whisk together dressing ingredients. Mix together nut topping ingredients, spread on baking sheet and bake at 350 degrees for 5-10 minutes. Cool.

To the salad mix, add the shredded chicken, the dressing, and the nut mixture. Toss well. Serve.

Soups, Stews & Eat-It-With-A-Fork Chowders

Cheddar Cheese Chowder

Contributed by Jim Grupa

Ingredients:

- **2 cups water**
- **2 cups peeled, diced potatoes**
- **½ cup peeled, diced carrots**
- **½ cup diced celery**
- **¼ cup chopped onion**
- **1 tsp. salt**
- **¼ tsp. pepper**
- **1 cup cooked, diced ham**
- **¼ cup butter**
- **¼ cup flour or cornstarch**
- **2 cups milk**
- **2 cups finely shredded cheddar cheese**

Directions:

In a large soup kettle combine water, potatoes, carrots, celery, onion, salt and pepper. Bring to a boil and boil for 15 minutes.

While this is cooking, melt butter in a smaller saucepan. Stir in flour or cornstarch until smooth. Gradually add milk and cook, stirring constantly until mixture is thickened. Add cheese and stir until cheese is melted. Fold in ham.

Add cooked vegetables (do not drain) and stir to blend. You may add more milk and beat thoroughly if you desire a thinner chowder.

Hot Sour Soup

My mouth is watering just typing this!

Contributed by Pat Staige (Phil's sister)

Ingredients:

- **6 medium dried black mushrooms**
- **1/4 to 1/2 lb. boneless pork loin**
- **1 Tbsp. cornstarch**
- **1/2 tsp. salt**
- **1 Tbsp. soy sauce**
- **6 ounces of firm bean curd (tofu)**
- **6 cups of chicken broth**
- **1/4 cup of vinegar**
- **2 Tbsp. soy sauce**
- **1 tsp. salt**
- **1/2 cup slivered canned bamboo shoots**
- **2 Tbsp. cornstarch**
- **2 Tbsp. cold water**
- **1/4 to 1 tsp. white pepper, depending upon your taste**
- **2 eggs, slightly beaten**
- **1/4 cup chopped green onions (with tops)**
- **2 tsp. oriental chili paste**
- **1/2 tsp. sesame oil**

Directions:

Soak mushrooms in warm water until soft, about 30 minutes; drain. Rinse in warm water; drain. Remove and discard stems; cut caps into thin slices.

Cut pork into thin slices. Toss pork, 1 tablespoon cornstarch, 1/2 teaspoon salt and 1 tablespoon soy sauce in a bowl. Cover and refrigerate 15 minutes.

Cut bean curd (tofu) into 1 1/2 x 1/4 pieces.

Heat chicken broth, vinegar, 2 tablespoons soy sauce and 1 teaspoon salt to boiling in large sauce pan. Stir in bamboo shoots, mushrooms, pork and bean curd. Cover and simmer 5 minutes.

Mix 2 tablespoons cornstarch, water and white pepper; stir into soup. Heat to boiling, stirring constantly.

Pour egg slowly into soup, stirring constantly with fork or whisk until egg forms shreds. Stir in green onions, pepper sauce and sesame oil.

This can serve up to 8 people, but with me, it would serve me and a couple others.

(I have also made a variation by adding 1/2 cup of baby shrimp.)

Hamburger Veggie Soup

Contributed by Pam & Dan Callahan
(Ph'riends of a ph'riend, Doug MacLennan)

Ingredients:

- **1 lb. ground beef**
- **1 10-ounce package frozen mixed veggies**
- **2 cups potato (diced)**
- **1 cup carrot (sliced)**
- **1 cup onion (chopped)**
- **1 14 1/2-ounce can tomatoes (undrained)**
- **4 cubes beef bouillon**
- **4 cups water**
- **1 Tbsp. garlic**
- **1/2 tsp. seasoning salt**
- **1/4 tsp. black pepper**
- **1/4 tsp. basil**
- **1 bay leaf**

Directions:

In large kettle, brown ground beef, sprinkle w/salt. Stir in remaining ingredients. Bring to boil, simmer, covered, approximately 30 minutes.

Cook's Tip!

Parsley is a garlic magnet! When you overdo the garlic in a soup or sauce, place a few parsley flakes in a tea ball to soak up the excess garlic.

Hearty Hash Brown Soup

Contributed by Jim Grupa
Adapted from: Taste of Home 2000

Ingredients:

- **2 lbs. frozen hash brown potatoes**
- **4 cups water**
- **1 large onion, chopped**
- **¾ cup sliced celery**
- **4 chicken bouillon**
- **½ tsp. celery seed**
- **¼ tsp. pepper**

- **4 cans (10 ¾ ounces each) condensed Cream of Chicken soup, undiluted**
- **1 quart milk**
- **2 cups cubed fully cooked ham**
- **1 Tbsp. dried parsley flakes**
- **1½ tsp. garlic salt**
- **8 bacon strips, cooked and crumbled**

Directions:

In a Dutch oven or soup kettle, combine the first seven ingredients; bring to a boil.

Reduce heat; cover and simmer for 20 minutes or until vegetables are tender. Mash vegetables with cooking liquid.

Add soup and milk; stir until smooth.

Add ham, parsley and garlic salt; simmer for 10 minutes or until heated through.

Garnish with bacon.

Yield: 12-16 servings (4 quarts).

Grand Casino Hinckley's Wild Rice Soup

Contributed by Helen Sheldon
(Phil's aunt)

Ingredients:

- **1 cup cooked wild rice**
- **1/4 tsp. poultry seasoning**
- **1/4 cup butter**
- **1/2 tsp. white pepper**
- **2 cups diced celery**
- **1 1/4 cup flour**
- **1/2 cup diced onions**
- **6 cups cold water**
- **1/2 cup shredded carrots**
- **1/4 tsp. Kitchen Bouquet seasoning**
- **8 oz. sliced mushrooms**
- **12 oz. diced cooked chicken, white meat**
- **5 1/2 tsp. chicken base**
- **2 1/4 cup whipping cream**
- **1 l/2 tsp. Nature's seasoning**
- **Fresh parsley - about 2 tsp.**

Directions:

In large kettle, melt butter and saute celery, carrots, onion, spices, seasoning and chicken base. When veggies are almost done, add mushrooms. Saute about 5 minutes more.

Slowly add flour until incorporated into vegetable mixture. Slowly add cold water and stir until there are no lumps.

Add chicken and rice and heat until thermometer registers 180 degrees. Add heavy cream and return to 180 degrees. (Do not boil.)

Garnish with parsley and enjoy!

Chicken Wild Rice Soup

Here's a less-famous version with a bit of bacon to boot ...

Contributed by Molly Babbitt
(Ph'riend of a ph'riend)

Ingredients:

- **4 small chicken breasts**
- **8 slices of bacon**
- **3 cans of chicken broth**
- **2 cups water**
- **1 cup wild rice**
- **1/2 chopped onion**
- **1/2 cup butter**
- **3/4 cup flour**
- **1/2 tsp. salt**
- **1/4 tsp. poultry season**
- **1/8 tsp. pepper**
- **1 pint of half and half**
- **Chopped mushrooms (optional)**

Directions:

Cook the chicken, chop into small pieces.

Cook the bacon, chop into bits and mix with the chicken.

Add all the other ingredients to the meat in a stock pot, boil, reduce heat, and cook for about 40 minutes. I usually simmer the soup without a cover. The longer the soup simmers, the thicker it gets. Yum! Yum!

New England Clam Chowder

Contributed by Jim Grupa

Ingredients:

- **1 pint shucked clams or 2 6½ oz. cans minced clams**
- **2 slices bacon, halved**
- **2 ½ cups finely chopped, peeled potatoes**
- **1 cup chopped onion**
- **1 tsp. instant chicken bouillon granules**
- **1 tsp. worcestershire sauce**
- **¼ tsp. dried thyme, crushed**
- **1/8 tsp. pepper**
- **2 cups milk**
- **1 cup light cream**
- **2 Tbsp. all-purpose flour**

Directions:

Chop shucked clams, reserving juice; set clams aside. Strain clam juice to remove bits of shell. (Or, if using canned clams, drain and reserve juice.) If necessary, add water to clam juice to equal 1 cup. Set clam-juice mixture aside.

In a large saucepan, cook bacon till crisp. Remove bacon, reserving 1 tablespoon drippings. Drain bacon on paper towels; crumble. Set aside.

In the same saucepan combine reserved bacon drippings, reserved clam-juice mixture, potatoes, onion, bouillon granules, worcestershire sauce, thyme and pepper. Bring to boiling; reduce heat. Cover and simmer for about 10 minutes or until potatoes are tender.

With a fork, mash potatoes slightly against the side of the pan.

Combine milk, cream and flour till smooth. Add to potato mixture. Cook and stir till slightly thickened and bubbly.

Stir in clams. Return to boiling; reduce heat. Cook 1 to 2 minutes more.

Sprinkle each serving with some of the crumbled bacon.

Makes 4 main-dish servings or 6 to 8 side-dish servings.

Fish Chowder. Prepare New England Clam Chowder as above, except substitute 1 pound fresh or frozen fish steaks; cut ¾ inch thick, for the clams.

Thaw fish, if frozen, and cut into ¾-inch cubes.

Substitute 1 cup water for the reserved clam juice and add ½ cup sliced carrot with potatoes and onion.

Add fish to chowder with milk mixture. Bring just to boiling; reduce heat. Cover, simmer about 3 minutes or till fish flakes easily with a fork.

Cook's Tip!

If dried herbs have lost their flavor and intensity, crush them before using and soak them for a few seconds in hot water.

White Bean and Pork Chili

Contributed by Jane Palmer

Ingredients:

- **3 Tbsp. olive oil**
- **1 medium onion chopped**
- **2 medium carrots chopped**
- **2 medium celery stalks chopped**
- **2 large garlic cloves minced**
- **1 lb. pork, cut into ½ inch cubes**
- **Salt and freshly ground pepper**
- **1 tsp. chili powder (or to taste)**
- **½ tsp. cumin**
- **½ tsp. dried oregano, crumbled**
- **1/8 tsp. ground sage**
- **1 cup beef broth**
- **1 (14/12 oz) can peeled tomatoes, undrained**
- **2 (15 oz) cans great northern or cannelloni beans, rinsed and drained**
- **Grated cheddar cheese and/or Monterey Jack cheese**
- **Minced fresh cilantro (optional)**

Directions:

Heat 2 tablespoons olive oil in heavy saucepan over medium-low heat. Add onion, carrots, celery and garlic and cook until tender, about 10 minutes.

Meanwhile, heat remaining 1 tablespoon oil in heavy large skillet over high heat. Pat pork dry. Add to skillet, season with salt and pepper and cook until browned, stirring frequently, about 6 minutes. Add pork to vegetables. Blend in spices and stir 3 minutes. Add broth and tomatoes with liquid and bring to boil.

Reduce heat, cover and simmer until pork is tender, stirring occasionally, approx. 1 hour. Add beans to mixture and heat through. Top with cheese and cilantro.

Karen's Ph'amous Chili

Contributed by Karen Staige
(Phil's wi'phe)

Ingredients:

- **1 lb. hamburger**
- **1 packet hot chili mix**
- **1 28 oz. canned tomatoes, whole or crushed**
- **1 8 oz. can tomato paste**
- **1 to 2 drops liquid smoke**
- **1 to 2 cans red kidney beans**

Directions:

Brown hamburger, drain fat and add chili mix and a little water. Let simmer for 5 minutes.

Add tomatoes, tomato paste and beans; heat thoroughly.

Add liquid smoke and let simmer. The longer it simmers; the better the flavor.

We have lots of fun adding different spices depending on who's eating it ... our children or John and Rose Mary!

Wisconsin Beer Cheese Soup

Contributed by Jim Grupa

Ingredients:

- **10 Tbsp. butter**
- **1/2 cup minced celery**
- **1/2 cup grated carrots**
- **1/2 cup finely chopped onion**
- **1/2 cup flour**
- **4-1/2 cups chicken broth**
- **1 12-ounce can of beer**
- **12 ounces sharp cheddar, grated**
- **2 Tbsp. Parmesan cheese**
- **1/2 tsp. dry mustard**

Directions:

Melt butter in a heavy pot over low heat. Saute vegetables until limp. Stir in flour and stir over low heat until flour expands.

Gradually add broth, stirring constantly until thickened. Simmer 5 minutes.

Add beer and stir. Gradually whisk in cheeses. Add seasoning. Simmer 7 minutes. Do not boil.

Serves 6 to 8.

Note: Cheddar cheese can be half white cheddar and half yellow cheddar.

Chicken Tortilla Soup

Contributed by Carol Saecker

Ingredients:

- **1 large onion, chopped**
- **1 tsp. cumin seed, lightly crushed**
- **1 Tbsp. olive oil**
- **4 ½ cups chicken broth**
- **1 can Mexican-style tomatoes**
- **½ cup fresh cilantro, snipped**
- **2 Tbsp. fresh lime juice**
- **1 ½ to 2 cups cooked chicken, shredded**

Directions:

In a large saucepan, cook onion and cumin seed in hot oil until onion is tender. Add broth, tomatoes, cilantro and lime juice. Bring to boil, reduce heat and simmer covered for 10 minutes. Add chicken. Cook until heated through. Ladle soup into bowls and top with tortilla strips.

Tortilla Strips:

- **5 small corn tortillas**
- **cooking oil**
- **Salt and pepper**

Using a pastry brush, brush some oil on both sides of one tortilla. Sprinkle with salt and pepper. Place another tortilla on top of first one and brush the top side with oil and season with salt and pepper. Repeat with remaining tortillas. With pizza cutter or large knife cut the stacked tortillas in half. Take one of the stacks and cut into thin strips. Repeat with other stack. Spread strips on cookie sheet and bake in 350 degree oven for 8 minutes or until crisp.

Spicy Cheeseburger Soup

Contributed by Jim Grupa
Adapted from Taste of Home 2000

Ingredients:

- **1 ½ cups water**
- **2 cups cubed peeled potatoes**
- **2 small carrots, grated**
- **1 small onion, chopped**
- **¼ cup chopped green pepper**
- **1 jalapeno pepper, seeded and chopped**
- **1 garlic clove, minced**
- **1 Tbsp. beef bouillon granules**
- **½ tsp. salt**

- **1 lb. ground beef, cooked and drained**
- **2½ cups milk, divided**
- **3 Tbsp. all-purpose flour**
- **8 ounces process American cheese, cubed**
- **¼ to 1 tsp. cayenne pepper, optional**
- **½ lb. sliced bacon, cooked and crumbled**

Directions:

In a large saucepan, combine the first nine ingredients; bring to a boil. Reduce heat; cover and simmer for 15 – 20 minutes or until potatoes are tender.

Stir in beef and 2 cups of milk; heat through.

Combine flour and remaining milk until smooth; gradually stir into soup. Bring to a boil; cook and stir for 2 minutes or until thickened and bubbly.

Reduce heat; stir in cheese until melted. Add cayenne if desired. Top with bacon just before serving.

Veggie Cheese Soup

Contributed by Karen Howe

Ingredients:

- **4 cubes chicken bouillon**
- **6 cups water**
- **1½ cups diced potatoes**
- **1 cup diced carrots**
- **1 cup celery (chopped)**
- **½ cup chopped onion**
- **1 pkg. frozen cauliflower (16 oz.)**
- **2 cans Cream of Chicken soup (10.5 oz. cans)**
- **1 lb. Velveeta**

Directions:

Dissolve bouillon into water.

Add fresh vegetables. Cook 15 minutes.

Add frozen vegetables. Cook 8 minutes.

Add soup and cheese. Cook until smooth.

Cook's Tip!

To keep a pot from boiling over, place a wooden spoon across the top of the uncovered pot!

Chicken and Corn Chowder with Thyme

Contributed by Jim Grupa
Adapted from www.epicurious.com

Ingredients:

- **3 slices bacon, chopped**
- **1 medium onion, chopped**
- **1 14 ½ -ounce can low-salt chicken broth**
- **1 10- to 12-ounce russet potato, peeled, and cut into ½-inch pieces**
- **2 cups corn kernels, fresh or frozen (about one 10-ounce package frozen)**
- **6 to 8 ounces boneless chicken thighs, cut into ½-inch pieces (about 1 cup)**
- **2 Tbsp. chopped fresh thyme or 1 ½ tsp. dried**
- **1 cup half and half**

Directions:

Cook bacon in heavy large saucepan over medium-high heat until brown and crisp, about 5 minutes. Using slotted spoon, transfer bacon to paper towels and drain. Discard all but 2 tablespoons drippings from pan.

Add onion; sauté until beginning to soften, about 3 minutes. Add broth and potato. Cover pan; simmer 5 minutes.

Add corn, chicken and thyme. Partially cover pan; simmer until chicken is cooked through and vegetables are tender, about 8 minutes. Add half and half and bring to simmer, about 2 minutes. Season chowder to taste with salt and pepper. Ladle into bowls. Serve with a sprinkle of cooked bacon.

Yield: 2 servings.

Beef Stew

Contributed by Lynn Johnson & "Big Jer"
(Phil's cousin)

Ingredients:

- **2 lbs. beef stew meat (venison can be substituted)**
- **3 potatoes**
- **6 carrots**
- **1 onion**
- **3 celery stalks**
- **1 16-ounce can tomatoes**
- **2 tsp. salt**
- **1 Tbsp. sugar**
- **3 Tbsp. Tapioca (minute)**

Directions:

Chop up everything into bite-sized pieces and cook, covered, for 5 hours in 250 degree oven.

Cook's Tip!

When boiling corn on the cob, add a little milk to the water to bring out the sweetness.

White Chili

Contributed by Lynn Johnson & "Big Jer"
(Phil's cousin)

Ingredients:

- **1 Tbsp. vegetable oil**
- **1 lb. skinless chicken breast, chopped and browned**
- **1 ¼ cup chopped onions**
- **2 cloves garlic, minced**
- **2 15-ounce great northern beans**
- **1 7-ounce Ortega diced chilies**
- **4 cans chicken broth**
- **2 Tbsp. Ortega jalapenos (opt.)**
- **2 tsp. ground cumin**
- **½ tsp. oregano**
- **1 ½ cups Monterey Jack shredded cheese**
- **½ cup sour cream**

Directions:

In Dutch oven, combine chicken, onions, garlic, beans, chilies, chicken broth, jalapenos, and spices. Stir to simmer. Fold in cheese and sour cream. Stir until melted.

Auntie Do Do's Chili

Contributed by Lynn Johnson & "Big Jer" (Phil's cousin)

Ingredients:

- **3 strips bacon, diced and browned**
- **1 lb. hamburger, browned and drained**
- **2 tsp. salt**
- **¼ tsp. pepper**
- **2 chopped onions**
- **1 cup celery, chopped**
- **1 Tbsp. chili powder**
- **3 cups canned tomatoes (no. 2 can)**
- **1 can kidney beans**
- **1 can mushrooms**
- **Garlic, to taste**
- **Small can of tomato paste**

Directions:

Combine bacon, hamburger, salt, pepper, onions, celery, chili powder and tomatoes. Simmer for 1 hour 15 minutes. Add remaining ingredients and serve.

Chili Bang-Bang

Contributed by Joan Staige

Ingredients:

- **2-3 lbs. ground beef**
- **1 large onion, chopped**
- **1 large can tomato juice**
- **1 can tomato soup**
- **1 can diced tomatoes**
- **2 cans Bushes chili beans**
- **1 Tbsp. sugar**
- **1 plain Hershey bar (optional)**
- **2 pkgs. Chili seasoning mix (Schilling)**

Directions:

Brown hamburger with the onion. Add the seasoning mixes and stir. Add the rest of the ingredients and simmer for 45 minutes.

Breads, Sweet Rolls & Diet-Busting Muph'ins!

Pumpkin Bread

Contributed by Jane Palmer

Ingredients:

Dry:

- **1 ½ cups sugar**
- **1 tsp. baking powder**
- **½ tsp. soda**
- **½ tsp. salt**
- **½ tsp. cinnamon**
- **½ tsp. cloves**
- **1 2/3 cups flour**
- **½ tsp. nutmeg**

Wet:

- **2 eggs**
- **1 cup pumpkin**
- **1/2 cup vegetable oil**

Directions:

Blend dry ingredients together.

Beat in eggs, pumpkin and vegetable oil.

Mix well and add dry ingredients.

Bake at 325 degrees.

Makes 2 small pans.

Double recipe and use 1 can pumpkin.

Bake approx 45 minutes. (1 hour for bigger pan.)

Sky High Popovers

Contributed by Florence Grupa

Ingredients:

- **3 eggs**
- **1 cup milk**
- **1 cup flour**
- **3 Tbsp. margarine, melted**
- **Dash of salt**

Directions:

Combine ingredients in blender for 30 seconds. Fill 6-8 well-greased custard cups or popover pan, ½ full.

Bake in preheated oven at 375 degrees for approximately 40 minutes until golden brown.

Energy Muph'ins

Contributed by Jane Palmer

Ingredients:

- **½ cup brown sugar**
- **¼ cup melted margarine or butter**
- **1 cup sour cream**
- **2 large eggs**
- **1 tsp. baking soda**
- **1 tsp. cinnamon**
- **1 ½ cup flour**
- **½ cup coconut**
- **½ cup raisins**
- **1 cup finely shredded carrots**

Directions:

In mixing bowl, combine sugar, butter, sour cream and eggs. Beat until smooth and creamy. Sift together soda, cinnamon and flour. Sift again over creamed mixture. Add coconut, raisins and carrots. Stir until all is well-blended and moist. Spoon into 12 paper-lined or greased and floured muffin tin cups, filling 2/3 full. Bake at 375 degrees for 15 to 20 minutes.

Variation: Bake in 2 small 3x5 inch loaf pans at 375 degrees for 30 minutes or 1 large 9x5 inch loaf pan for 45 minutes. Test for doneness. Ovens vary.

Cook's Tip!

For a recipe that includes cut up raisins, soak the knife in cold water for 10 minutes and the raisins will not stick when chopping!

Mom's Zucchini Bread

Contributed by Jean Baker

Ingredients:

- **3 eggs**
- **2 cups sugar**
- **1 cup salad oil**
- **2 tsp. vanilla 2 cups shredded zucchini (unpeeled)**
- **1 cup well drained crushed pineapple**
- **1 cup chopped nuts**
- **3 cups flour**
- **2 tsp. soda**
- **1 tsp. salt**
- **1 1/2 tsp. cinnamon**
- **1/2 tsp. baking powder**
- **3/4 tsp. nutmeg**
- **1 cup raisins or currents**

Directions:

Beat eggs, oil, sugar, and vanilla until foamy. Stir in zucchini and pineapple.

Combine flour, soda, salt, baking powder, cinnamon, nutmeg, nuts and raisins or currents. Stir gently into first mixture and stir until just blended.

Bake in 2 greased and floured 5 x 8 inch loaf pans at 350 degrees for 1 hour; test with toothpick.

Cool 10 minutes and remove from pans.

Maple Bar Muph'ins

If you like bakery-fresh maple bars (sometimes called Long John's), give these a try!

Contributed by Susan Carter

Combine in mixing bowl:

- **3 cups flour**
- **1 & 1/4 cups granulated sugar**
- **3/4 tsp. salt**
- **1 Tbsp. baking powder**
- **1 tsp. baking soda**

In separate bowl, combine and whisk until smooth:

- **3/4 cup buttermilk**
- **3/4 cup milk**
- **1/3 cup ricotta cheese**
- **3 Tbsp. vegetable oil**
- **1 large whole egg plus 2 egg whites**
- **2 Tbsp. vanilla extract**

Pour into dry ingredients and mix just until moist. Spoon batter into muffin/cupcake tins lined with paper muffin cups and sprayed with vegetable oil. Fill to the rims. Bake at 375 for 20 minutes or until a toothpick inserted into the center comes out clean. Cool completely in tins.

Beat until creamy and frost cooled muph'ins with:

- **1 & 3/4 cups powdered sugar**
- **1 & 1/4 tsp. maple extract**
- **2 Tbsp. cream cheese, room temperature**
- **1 tsp. vanilla extract**
- **Pinch of salt**
- **1 Tbsp. plus 2 tsp. water**

Polish Coffee Cake

Contributed by Florence Grupa

Ingredients:

- **½ cup margarine**
- **2 cups flour**
- **2 cups sugar**

- **1 cup flour**
- **3 beaten eggs**
- **¾ cup milk**
- **2 tsp. baking powder**
- **1 tsp. vanilla**

Directions:

Mix margarine, 2 cups flour and sugar with hands until the consistency of streusel. Set aside one cup.

To the remaining mixture, add 1 cup flour, eggs, milk, baking powder and vanilla.

Pour into greased loaf pan. Sprinkle remaining streusel on top.

Bake at 350 degrees for about 1 hour.

Banana Bread

Contributed by Helen Sheldon
(Phil's aunt)

Ingredients:

- **1/4 cup shortening**
- **1 cup granulated sugar**
- **2 eggs**
- **1 tsp. baking soda**
- **1 tsp. baking powder**
- **1/4 tsp. salt**
- **1 cup mashed bananas**
- **1/2 chopped nuts**
- **2 cups all purpose flour**

Directions:

This makes one large loaf. Grease pan well. Cream shortening and sugar together well. Add eggs and beat. Add mashed bananas and blend well. Sift flour, baking powder, soda and salt together and add to above mixture stirring only as much as needed to mix in flour. Do not beat. Put in prepared loaf pan and let sit for about 30 minutes. Bake for 1 hour at 350 degrees. Test for doneness. Tip out on wire rack to cool.

Cook's Tip!

To quickly ripen bananas, wrap in a wet paper towel and place in a brown-paper bag.

Jewish Coffee Cake

Contributed by Florence Grupa

For Dough:

Cream together:
- **½ cup butter**
- **1 cup sugar**

Add: 3 eggs

Beat well.

Add:
- **2 cups flour**
- **1 tsp. baking powder**
- **1 tsp. baking soda**
- **½ pint sour cream**
- **1/8 tsp. salt**
- **1 tsp. vanilla**

For Topping Combine:
- **¾ cups chopped nuts**
- **1 cup packed brown sugar**
- **3 Tbsp. flour**
- **3 Tbsp. butter**

Directions:

Grease and flour a torte or tube pan.

Put ½ of dough on bottom of pan and sprinkle with ½ of the topping. Put remaining dough in pan and sprinkle with the rest of the topping.

Bake at 350 degrees for 50-60 minutes.

Big Dog Sweet Rolls

"Even Junior Barnes likes 'em!"

Contributed by Allen Staige

Ingredients:

- **2 loaves frozen bread**
- **1 cup packed brown sugar**
- **½ cup butter**
- **1 tsp. cinnamon (heaping)**
- **2 Tbsp. milk**
- **Chopped nuts (optional)**

Directions:

Thaw bread dough. Cream together brown sugar, butter, cinnamon and milk. Cut one loaf into 12 pieces and place them in the bottom of a greased cake pan (9 x 13). Spoon creamed mixture over tops of dough, putting some in the empty spaces. Sprinkle nuts over the top. Cut second loaf into twelve (12) pieces and scatter them over the topping.

Cover and let rise until doubled. Bake at 375 degrees for 20-25 minutes.

Cook's Tip!

De-lump brown sugar by putting it in the microwave with a slice of fresh white bread, cover the dish tightly and heat for 15 to 20 seconds. Let stand for five minutes before using.

Monkey Bread

Contributed by Susan Fryer
(Phil's wi'phe's sister)

Ingredients:

- **1 tube of refrigerated biscuits**
- **1 1/2 cups brown sugar**
- **1 Tbsp. cinnamon**
- **1 1/2 sticks butter or margarine**

Directions:

Cut biscuits into quarters. Arrange half of them in a round cake pan.

Mix sugar and cinnamon together and sprinkle half over the first layer.

Melt butter, and pour 1/2 over biscuits.

Repeat procedure with the rest of biscuits.

Bake at 350 degrees for 30 minutes, best if served warm.

Pepperoni Bread

Contributed by Nick and Lori Edstrom

Ingredients:

- **1 loaf white frozen bread dough**
- **1 egg**
- **5-6 slices provolone cheese**
- **8-10 slices salami**
- **2 ounces sliced pepperoni**
- **1 4-ounce package mozzarella cheese, shredded**
- **Salt and pepper**
- **Oregano**
- **Parsley**
- **Onion powder**
- **Garlic powder**
- **1-2 tsp. olive oil**
- **Parmesan cheese, grated**

Directions:

Defrost dough on greased round cookie sheet. Spread until thin, drawing dough as close to edges as possible.

Beat egg and brush half of it over the dough.

Alternate salami, pepperoni, and provolone over dough. Sprinkle top with remaining ingredients.

Start at one edge and begin rolling like a jelly roll, covering dough with remaining egg after each turn. Seal ends and place seam side down on pan.

Bake at 325 degrees for 30-45 minutes.

Amaretto Cheese Danish

Contributed by Susan Carter

Danish Ingredients:

- **3 oz. cream cheese**
- **1/2 tsp. almond extract**
- **1/4 cup confectioners' sugar**
- **1 Tbsp. chopped almonds**
- **10 oz. can refrigerated pizza dough**
- **1 egg white mixed with 1/2 tsp. water**

Glaze:

- **1/2 cups confectioners sugar**
- **1/4 tsp. almond extract**
- **2 tsp. milk**

Directions:

Preheat oven to 425 degrees. Coat a cookie sheet with nonstick spray and set aside.

In a small bowl beat the cream cheese, almond extract and confectioners' sugar until smooth. Stir in chopped almonds and set aside.

Roll dough into a rectangle. Spread the cream cheese mixture over the dough to within 1/4-inch of the edges. Start at one end and roll up, firmly pinching the edges and ends to seal. Slice crosswise into 20 small cylindrical pieces. Place on prepared cookie sheets.

Brush egg/water mixture over rolls and bake for 12 minutes or until golden brown.

In a small bowl, blend the glaze ingredients until smooth. Drizzle over warm rolls. Serve warm.

Cheesy Sourdough Bread

Contributed by Pam and Dan Callahan
(Ph'riends of a ph'riend, Doug MacLennan)

Ingredients:

- **1 loaf sourdough bread (round)**
- **1 cup mayonnaise**
- **1 cup gruyére cheese (3 oz.)**
- **2 Tbsp. chives (fresh snipped)**
- **1-1/2 tsp. garlic (minced)**

Directions:

Slice loaf horizontally into three equal pieces. Arrange cut-side-up on baking sheet.

In small bowl, combine remaining ingredients. Spread mixture evenly to edge of each bread piece. Bake at 375 degrees until topping is puffy and golden brown (12-15 minutes).

Cut warm bread into wedges; serve immediately.

Ginger Cream Scones

Resist the urge to eat the scones hot out of the oven. Letting them cool for at least 10 minutes firms them up and improves their texture.

Contributed by Susan Carter

Ingredients:

- **2 cups (10 ounces) unbleached all-purpose flour**
- **1 Tbsp. baking powder**
- **3 Tbsp. sugar**
- **1/2 tsp. salt**
- **5 Tbsp. chilled unsalted butter, cut into 1/4-inch cubes**
- **1/2 cup crystallized ginger, diced**
- **1 cup heavy cream**

Directions:

Adjust oven rack to middle position and heat oven to 425 degrees.

Place flour, baking powder, sugar, and salt in workbowl of food processor fitted with steel blade. Pulse six times. Remove cover and distribute butter evenly over dry ingredients. Cover and pulse 12 times, each pulse lasting 1 second. Add crystallized ginger and pulse one more time. Transfer dough to large bowl. Stir in heavy cream with rubber spatula or fork until dough begins to form, about 30 seconds. Transfer dough and all dry, floury bits to countertop and knead dough by hand just until it comes together into a rough, slightly sticky ball, 5 to 10 seconds.

Flatten dough into 10-12 inch round and cut scones into 8 wedges (like you would a pie). Place wedges on cold, ungreased baking sheet. Bake until scone tops are light brown, 12 to 15 minutes. Cool on wire rack for at least 10 minutes. Serve warm or at room temperature.

Ph'rom Morning 'til Night Ph'abulous Main Events

Make-Ahead Breakfast Casserole

Contributed by Jane Palmer

Ingredients:

- **2 ½ cups seasoned croutons**
- **1 lb. pork sausage**
- **4 eggs**
- **2 ¼ cups milk**
- **1 (10 oz.) can cream of mushroom soup**
- **1 (10 oz.) pkg. frozen chopped spinach, thawed and squeezed dry**
- **1 (4 oz.) can mushrooms, drained and chopped**
- **1 cup (4 oz.) shredded sharp cheddar cheese**
- **1 cup (4 oz.) shredded Monterey Jack cheese**
- **¼ tsp. dry mustard**
- **Fresh herb sprigs and carrot strips (optional)**

Directions:

Spread croutons on bottom of greased 9 x 13 inch baking dish.

Crumble sausage into medium skillet. Cook over medium heat until browned, stirring occasionally. Drain off any drippings. Spread over croutons.

Whisk eggs and milk in large bowl until blended. Stir in soup, spinach, mushrooms, cheese and mustard. Pour egg mixture over sausage and croutons.

Refrigerate overnight.

Preheat oven to 325 degrees. Bake egg mixture 50-55 minutes or until set and lightly browned on top. Garnish with herb sprigs and carrot, if desired. Refrigerate leftovers. Makes 10-12 servings.

Aebleskiver (Danish Pancake Balls)

Here's one from my grandmother, Jennie Sorensen. I remember her making them with a slice of canned peach inside each ball of pancake.

Contributed by Linda Grupa

Ingredients:

- **1 1/2 cups of flour**
- **1 tsp. sugar**
- **1/2 tsp. salt**
- **1 tsp. baking power**
- **6 eggs, separated**
- **1 cup of milk**

Directions:

Sift together the flour, sugar, salt and baking powder.

In a separate mixing bowl beat the egg yolks well, then add the milk. Mix into this the dry ingredients that have been sifted together.

Beat egg whites till stiff, and carefully fold into batter.

In hot Aebleskiver pan put 1 1/2 teaspoon oil in each cup. Then spoon or pour in batter just to the top of each cup. Bake (fry) until delicately brown underneath, loosen around edges with fork, quickly turn and brown other side. Use cake tester to determine when done.

Be careful not to get your pan too hot as the aebleskiver burn easily.

Serve dipped in sugar or syrup, or good quality jam or jelly.

Cotter Band "Wake-Up" Egg Casserole

Contributed by Mary Wojciechowski

Ingredients:

- **7 pieces bread, cubed**
- **1 1/2 lb. Jimmy Dean sausage (original)**
- **I cup grated Cheddar cheese (sharp)**
- **5 eggs, mixed with 2 1/2 cups milk or 6 eggs, mixed with 2 3/4 cups milk**
- **Paprika**

Directions:

Butter 9 X 13 pan. Layer the bread, then the sausage, and top with the cheese. Beat egg and milk together and pour over all. Sprinkle paprika over all.

Bake at 350 degrees for 35 minutes.

Can be made the night before and covered with foil and refrigerated.

Grandpa Ted's Ph'rench Pancakes

Contributed by Ted Brink
(Karen's dad)

Ingredients:

- **4-6 eggs, beaten**
- **1/2 to 1 cup milk**
- **1/2 to 1 cup flour**
- **1/2 tsp. salt**

Directions:

Mix ingredients together.

Ladle batter into heavy skillet and fry in 2 tablespoons hot shortening until brown, or crisp around the edges. Turn pancake.

Pancake will curl up. When it goes down, it is done.

Cook's Tip!

For perfectly shaped pancakes, use a meat baster to "squeeze" pancake batter onto the hot griddle.

Ph'rench Pancakes

A slightly different version, adding a bit of spice and vanilla.

Contributed by Janet Staige-Stanton
(Phil's sister)

Ingredients:

- **1 cup sifted flour**
- **1/2 tsp. salt**
- **Dash of cinnamon**
- **1 cup milk**
- **3 eggs, separated**
- **2 Tbsp. melted butter**
- **1/4 tsp. vanilla**

Directions:

Sift flour, salt and cinnamon together.

In separate bowls, beat egg whites then yolks.

Add milk to beaten yolks, then add butter.

Stir in flour and then fold in egg whites, then add vanilla.

Heat non-stick griddle to 350 degrees.

Ladle approximately 1/4 cup of batter onto griddle, using the bottom of the ladle to spread pancake in a circular motion so pancake is slightly thinner than a typical pancake. Brown on both sides.

Top with melted butter and a generous sprinkle of powdered sugar and roll pancake like a cigar and eat.

Makes 6-8 pancakes.

Potato Pancakes

Contributed by Jean Baker

Ingredients:

- ***6 medium raw potatoes, grated***
- ***2 eggs, separated***
- ***1 Tbsp. grated onion***
- **Salt & pepper to taste**
- **Butter**

Directions:

Mix potatoes, egg yolks, onion, salt and pepper. Add a little flour if batter is too loose.

Beat egg whites until stiff. Fold into potato mixture.

Heat a little butter in frying pan. Drop tablespoons of mixture in pan. Fry until golden on both sides.

Serve with applesauce.

Cook's Tip!

Bit of yolk sneak into your egg white? Use a Q-tip or edge of a paper towel to draw any small bit of yolk out of egg whites before beating.

Overnight Baked Ph'rench Toast

Contributed by Susan Carter

Ingredients:

- **1 cup cream, half-and-half, or whole milk**
- **6 large eggs**
- **¼ cup maple syrup**
- **2 Tbsp. packed light brown sugar**
- **1 tsp. vanilla**
- **¼ tsp. salt**
- **8 slices bread, preferably a dense egg bread (challah)**

Directions:

Whisk all ingredients (except bread) together in an 8 x 8 inch baking dish.

Trim crusts from 8 slices white or egg (challah) bread. Coat each slice of bread in egg mixture, then fit bread into the pan in a double layer. Gently press the bread with the back of a fork to compress the slices slightly. Cover with plastic wrap and press the plastic against the top layer to help bread soak up egg mixture. Refrigerate overnight.

Preheat oven to 400 degrees. Lightly butter a baking sheet, preferably nonstick.

Use a wide spatula to lift each slice of bread from egg mix, allow excess to drip back into the pan, and place on baking sheet in single layer.

Bake until puffed and golden, 12 – 15 minutes, turning slices over halfway through baking. Serve with powdered sugar and maple syrup.

Maple Ph'rench Toast Bake

Contributed by Christina Staige

Ingredients:

- **12 slices bread, cubed**
- **1 package (8 oz.) cream cheese, cubed**
- **8 eggs**
- **1 cup milk**
- **½ cup maple syrup**
- **Additional maple syrup**

Directions:

Arrange half of the bread cubes in a greased shallow 2-qt. baking dish. Top with the cream cheese and remaining bread.

In a bowl, whisk eggs, milk and syrup. Pour over bread. Cover and refrigerate overnight.

Remove from the refrigerator 30 minutes before baking.

Cover and bake at 350 degrees for 30 minutes. Uncover and bake 20 – 25 minutes longer or until golden brown.

Serve with additional syrup.

8 servings

Sunday Brunch Eggs

Contributed by Susan Fryer

Ingredients:

- **8 pieces of buttered bread, torn into pieces**
- **4 eggs**
- **2 cups milk**
- **8 oz. shredded cheddar cheese**
- **1 pkg. breakfast sausages, cut into bite size pieces**
- **Salt and pepper**

Directions:

Mix all ingredients, refrigerate, and let set overnight.

Bake for 45 minutes at 350 degrees.

Cook's Tip!

Dampen your fingers a little before handling an egg and it will not slip away!

Potatoes Crust Quiche

Contributed by Bev Keiper

Ingredients:

CRUST:

- **4 cups coarsely shredded raw potatoes (about 4 large)**
- **½ cup diced onion**
- **1 egg, beaten**
- **1 cup of flour**
- **½ tsp. salt**

FILLING:

- **1 ½ cups (6-oz.) shredded Colby cheese, divided**
- **½ cup chopped onion**
- **1 ½ cups diced cooked ham (or other cooked meat)**
- **3 eggs, beaten**
- **1 cup light cream (I used milk)**
- **½ tsp. salt**
- **Dash of paprika, if desired**

Directions:

Combine crust ingredients and press into a well-greased 10-inch deep dish pie plate. Bake at 400 degrees for 20 minutes. Remove crust from oven; reduce heat to 350 degrees.

Add 1 cup cheese, onion, and ham to crust.

Mix eggs, cream, and salt. Pour onto cheese-onion-ham layer and sprinkle with paprika. Bake for 35-40 minutes until set.

Remove from the oven and top with remaining ½ cup of cheese. Let stand 5 minutes before serving.

Mom's Sausage Egg Bake

Contributed by Pam & Dan Callahan
(Ph'riends of a ph'riend, Doug MacLennan)

Ingredients:

- **2 rolls pork sausage (thawed)**
- **2 cups cheddar cheese (grated)**
- **3 cups crouton (small stuffing type)**
- **6 eggs**
- **1 10 3/4-ounce can Cream of Mushroom soup**
- **3 cups milk (2-1/2 + 1/2)**
- **3/4 tsp. dry mustard**

Directions:

Layer croutons in greased 9 x 13" pan, top with cheese.

Brown sausage, drain, add dry mustard, place over cheese.

Beat eggs with 2-1/2 cups milk, pour egg mixture over top. Cover and refrigerate overnight.

Dilute soup with 1/2 cup milk, heat and pour over egg mixture. Bake uncovered for 1-1/2 hours at 325 degrees until sets. Let sit for five minutes before cutting.

SERVING SUGGESTION: Ham loaf and au gratin potatoes.

Puffy Omelet with Shrimp and Creamy Parmesan Sauce

Contributed by Susan Carter

Ingredients:

- **3 eggs, separated**
- **3 Tbsp. water**
- **1 Tbsp. butter**
- **Salt and pepper to taste**
- **6-8 cooked shrimp**
- **1 Tbsp. fresh dill, snipped (optional)**

Directions:

In small bowl, beat egg whites until stiff but not dry. In a separate bowl, beat egg yolks until thick and lemon colored, 2-3 minutes. Beat in water, salt and pepper. Gently fold egg mixture into egg whites with rubber spatula.

Melt butter in an 8 or 10 inch skillet on medium heat. When it begins to sizzle, rotate skillet to evenly coat bottom, then pour in omelet mixture. Gently level the surface.

Cover and cook undisturbed for 5 minutes. Omelet will puff up while cooking and edges will turn light brown. Remove from heat (omelet will deflate), arrange shrimp on one side of omelet, sprinkle with 1/2 the dill and 2 tablespoons of parmesan sauce (recipe below). Using a spatula, flip plain side of omelet over filled side, and slide onto plate. Serve with additional sauce and pinch of dill over the top.

Creamy Parmesan Sauce (makes about 1 cup):

- **½ cup cream**
- **1 cup grated parmesan**

Heat the cream (in microwave or on stove) until not but not boiling. Add the parmesan, stir until smooth.

Pepper Steak

Contributed by Jean Baker

Ingredients:

- **2 lbs. chuck roast (cut in strips)**
- **2 cups water**
- **2 beef bouillon cubes**
- **2 red and green peppers**
- **3 Tbsp. cornstarch**
- **2 Tbsp. soy sauce**
- **1/2 cup water**

Directions:

Brown meat in 3 tablespoons hot shortening, then add water and bouillon cubes, bring to a boil. Cover and simmer about 1 hour or until meat is tender.

Add peppers cut in eighths. Simmer 5 minutes.

Blend cornstarch, soy sauce and water. Add this to meat mixture and cook until thickened.

Serve with cooked rice and additional soy sauce if desired.

Grandma's Baked Chicken and Rice

Contributed by Carol Saecker

Ingredients:

- **6 chicken breast halves or 8 chicken thighs**
- **1 ¼ cups rice**
- **1 can beef consommé**
- **1 envelope dry onion soup mix**
- **1 can Cream of Mushroom soup**
- **1 cup water**

Directions:

Place rice in 9 X 13 inch baking dish, pour beef consommé over rice. Dip chicken pieces in dry onion soup mix and lay them on top of rice. Mix mushroom soup and water and pour over the chicken and rice.

Bake uncovered for 1 hour at 350 degrees and then cover with aluminum foil, reduce heat to 325 and bake for 30 minutes. Remove foil last 5 minutes to dry out the rice for serving.

Cook's Tip!

To tenderize and improve taste, submerge chickens in buttermilk and refrigerate for two to three hours before cooking.

Seafood Crepes

Contributed by Carol Saecker

Ingredients:

Crepes:

- **1 ½ cups milk**
- **3 eggs**
- **1 cup flour**
- **1/8 tsp. salt**

Filling:

- **Can of Cream of Mushroom soup**
- **½ cup milk**
- **1 cup Monterey Jack cheese, shredded**
- **4 oz. can mushrooms, drained**
- **8 oz. small cooked shrimp or 6 oz. can salmon, drained and flaked**
- **Steamed broccoli spears or asparagus spears**

Directions:

Crepes: Place milk, eggs, flour and salt in blender. Blend until smooth. Over medium heat, heat 12 inch non-stick skillet. When hot, brush lightly with peanut oil. Add approximately ¼ cup batter to skillet, rotating pan to spread batter evenly. Cook until surface is fairly set and edges are golden brown. Turn over with a quick flip and cook other side for a few seconds. Do not over cook or crepes will become hard and brittle and difficult to roll. Remove from pan, and stack. Repeat with remaining batter, brushing pan with additional oil as needed. Keep hot until serving time.

Filling: In saucepan over medium heat mix together soup and milk, stirring until mixed well. Add cheese, stirring until cheese melts. Add mushrooms and seafood. Heat through.

To serve, spoon about ½ cup seafood mixture down center of each crepe and sprinkle with paprika. Place steamed spears on top of mixture and roll up. Sprinkle with additional paprika. Serve.

Taco Hot Dish

Contributed by Carol Saecker

Ingredients:

- **1 lb. ground beef**
- **15 oz. can tomato sauce**
- **1 envelope taco seasoning mix**
- **15 oz. can refried beans**
- **2 ½ cups tortilla chips or corn chips**
- **½ cup shredded cheddar cheese**

Directions:

Brown ground beef, drain.

Add tomato sauce, taco seasoning and refried beans. Mix well.

In bottom of 2-quart casserole, put in 2 cups of the chips, breaking up slightly, if large. Cover with meat mixture.

Cover and bake at 375 degrees for 25 minutes.

Top with the cheddar cheese and remaining chips that have been crushed. Bake uncovered 5 minutes more.

Hot Beef Sandwich

Contributed by Sharon Woychek

Ingredients:

- **3 lbs. beef stew meat**
- **1 pkg. dry onion soup**
- **1 can Cream of Celery soup**

Directions:

Combine all in covered baking dish.

Bake 275 degrees for 5-6 hours.

Break meat with fork after 4 hours.

Serve on buns.

Serves 6-8 people.

Big Bob's Smoked Chicken with White BBQ Sauce

This recipe is especially for Phil, as he provided me with a lifetime supply of woodchips the last time I saw him. Besides that, it gets high marks from guests at the Baxter household.

Contributed by Bill Baxter
Source: Food and Wine Magazine
Recipe from Big Bob Gibson, Big Bob Gibson Bar-B-Q in Decatur AL

Ingredients:

- **2 whole chickens — 2 lbs. each**
- **2 tsp. kosher salt**
- **1 1/2 tsp. coarsely ground pepper**
- **1 1/2 tsp. light brown sugar**
- **1 1/2 tsp. paprika**
- **1 tsp. garlic powder**
- **1 tsp. onion powder**

White Barbecue Sauce:

- **1 cup mayonnaise**
- **3 Tbsp. cider vinegar**
- **2 Tbsp. prepared horseradish**
- **2 Tbsp. water**
- **1 tsp. kosher salt**
- **1/2 tsp. black pepper — freshly ground**
- **1/4 tsp. cayenne pepper**

Directions:

Soak the hickory chips in cold water for 1 hour. In a small bowl combine the salt and pepper with the brown sugar, paprika, garlic powder and the onion powder.

Light a grill, using the indirect method.

Drain the hickory chips and, if using a charcoal grill, scatter them on the hot coals. If using gas, place the chips in a 12 inch square of aluminum foil; then fold the foil into a 6 inch square package and poke 12 holes in the top. Place the package near the gas flame. Let the chips heat on high until smoking. If using a smoker, follow the maker's instructions.

Sprinkle 2 teaspoons of the spice mixture into the cavity of each chicken. Sprinkle the rest on the skin, and rub it in thoroughly. Set the chickens on the grill, breast side up, away from the heat. Cover and grill for 1 1/4 to 1 1/2 hours over medium heat, until an instant-read thermometer inserted inside the thickest part of the thigh reads 160 or until the skin is golden crisp and the juices run clear.

Transfer the chickens to a platter, and allow them to rest for 10 minutes.

Combine all of the White Barbeque sauce ingredients in a bowl, and whisk until smooth. Serve in a bowl on the side.

Yeilds 8 servings.

Bolognese-Style Meat Ragu

This recipe is straight from Italy, handed to us on the tour Martha and I took there. I know, part of it is metric measures, and it takes all day to make. Just be adventurous and get out the conversion book. There will be no complaints at the dinner table, I assure you!

Contributed by Bill Baxter
Source: "Sarah Nardone, tour guide extraordinaire"

Ingredients:

- **3 Tbsp. butter**
- **1 medium onion — finely chopped**
- **3 stalks celery — finely diced**
- **100 grams carrot — finely diced**
- **300 grams veal — ground**
- **250 grams pork — ground**
- **250 milliliters heavy cream**
- **250 milliliters white wine**
- **250 milliliters water**
- **440 grams Italian plum tomato — chopped**
- **1 Tbsp. Italian parsley — minced**
- **1/4 tsp. nutmeg — ground**
- **1 tsp. salt**
- **1/4 tsp. pepper**
- **1 lb. spaghetti**

Directions:

Heat the butter in a deep, heavy sauce pan and fry the onion over medium-high heat until translucent. Add the celery and carrot, continue cooking for 2 minutes.

Turn up the heat to high and add the ground veal and pork, the salt and pepper, and cook until all liquid has evaporated breaking up the meat as it cooks.
Stir in the heavy cream, and reduce heat to low, stirring

occasionally until the liquid has evaporated. Add the nutmeg and stir.

Add the wine, stirring occasionally until it has evaporated, then add the tomatoes with the tomato liquid and 250 ml. of water. Reduce heat to lowest setting and barely simmer for 2-3 hours, stirring occasionally and adding water as needed. By the end, the full-flavored oil should separate from the ragu', and the liquid should have boiled away.

Add the parsley, taste, and adjust the salt and pepper. Cook the pasta, remembering not to rinse after cooking. Toss the ragu with the pasta rather than pouring on top. The ragu can be enhanced at the end with some finely chopped chicken livers, or perhaps some mushrooms.

Use only freshly grated Italian parmigiano on the top.

Yield: 6 servings

Metric to U.S. Conversion Chart

Weight	Capacity
1 gram = .035 ounce	1 militers = 1/5 teaspoon
100 grams = 3.5 ounces	5 ml = 1 teaspoon
500 grams = 1.10 pounds	15 ml = 1 tablespoon
1 kilogram = 2.205 pounds	30 ml = 1 fluid oz.
1 kilogram = 35 oz.	100 ml = 3.4 fluid oz.
	240 ml = 1 cup
	1 liter = 34 fluid oz.
	1 liter = 4.2 cups
	1 liter = 2.1 pints
	1 liter = 1.06 quarts
	1 liter = .26 gallon

Cook's Tip!

Easily convert grams to ounces by multiplying grams by .035; multiply milliliters by .034 to get fluid ounces.

Mediterranean Ph'lounder

Contributed by Jane Palmer

Ingredients:

- **1 lb. flounder fillets**
- **1 thinly sliced small onion**
- **1 (14 ½ ounce) can diced tomatoes with basil, garlic and oregano with juice**
- **1/3 cup sliced black olives**
- **½ tsp. dried basil**
- **½ cup crumbled garlic-and-herb feta cheese**

Directions:

Heat oven to 425 degrees.

In a 9 by 13 inch baking dish, layer flounder, then onion.

Spoon tomatoes and olives evenly over flounder, then sprinkle with basil and cheese.

Bake, uncovered, 25 minutes or until fish is opaque.

Makes 4 servings.

Short-Cut Paella

Contributed by Jane Palmer

Ingredients:

- **1 Tbsp. olive oil**
- **½ cup chopped onion**
- **8 ounces smoked sausage or chorizo, cut lengthwise in half, then into ¼ inch slices**
- **1 cup rice**
- **2 tsp. Italian seasoning**
- **½ tsp. turmeric**
- **2 cups fat-free chicken broth**
- **1 14 ½ ounce can drained diced tomatoes**
- **1 lb. uncooked shrimp, thawed, peeled and deveined**
- **1 cup frozen peas**
- **Freshly ground black pepper**

Directions:

Heat oil in a large nonstick skillet on medium. Add onion and sausage, then cook 3 minutes or until onion is softened. Stir in rice, Italian seasoning and turmeric, then cook 2 minutes. Add broth, and bring to a boil. Cover, and simmer 15 minutes. Stir in tomatoes.

Place shrimp in a single layer on top of rice, then top with peas. Cover and cook on medium-low heat for 8 to 10 minutes or until rice is tender and shrimp are cooked. Season to taste with black pepper. Stir and serve.

Makes 6 servings.

Cuban Shrimp and Rice

Contributed by Jane Palmer

Ingredients:

- **2 Tbsp. oil**
- **½ cup chopped green pepper**
- **1/2 cup chopped onion**
- **1/2 tsp. salt**
- **Dash black pepper**
- **½ tsp. oregano**
- **½ tsp. cumin powder**
- **28 oz. canned tomatoes, stewed and peeled**
- **2 bay leaves (remove before serving)**
- **Garlic to taste**
- **1 lb. shrimp**

Directions:

Saute onions and pepper in oil. Add remaining ingredients. Bring to boil. Cook slowly covered about 15 minutes.

Add 1 lb shrimp. Bring to boil, simmer about 3 minutes until shrimp are done.

Serve over plain cooked white rice.

Serves 4-5.

Parmesan Chicken

Contributed by Jane Palmer

Ingredients:

- **1 ¼ cups seasoned bread crumbs (Italian)**
- **¼ cup grated Parmesan cheese**
- **2 Tbsp. Italian seasoning or parsley**
- **8 oz. boneless, skinless chicken breast halves**
- **1/3 cup Dijon mustard**

Directions:

Heat oven to 450 degrees.

Combine bread crumbs, Parmesan and Italian seasoning together in a bowl. Brush chicken with mustard; roll into seasoned bread crumb mixture and coat both sides.

Place chicken on a foil-lined pan. Bake at 450 degrees for 20 minutes or until chicken is fork tender and juices run clear.

Serves 8.

Cook's Tip!

To effortlessly skin a chicken, partially freeze it first.

Pizza Hotdish

Contributed by Rose Mary Staige

Ingredients:

- **1 16-oz. bag extra wide egg noodles (cooked)**
- **1 lb. hamburger (browned)**
- **1 small onion chopped (optional)**
- **1 can Cream of Cheddar soup (10 ¾ oz.) (substitute Nacho soup for more spice)**
- **2 15-oz. cans pizza sauce**
- **8-ounce bag shredded mozzarella cheese**

Directions:

Mix noodles, hamburger, onion, soup, and pizza sauce together and put in a buttered 9 x 13 inch pan.

Bake at 350 degrees for 40 minutes.

Top with 8 oz. bag shredded mozzarella cheese and bake an additional 10 minutes.

Let stand 10 minutes prior to serving.

Palpettos

Contributed by Karen Staige
(Phil's wi'phe)

Ingredients:

- **1 lb. shrimp**
- **1 cup bread crumbs**
- **1/2 cup parmesan cheese**
- **2 eggs**
- **Onion (chopped)**
- **Garlic**
- **Oil**
- **Salt**
- **Pepper**

Directions:

Beat eggs, onion, garlic, salt and pepper.

Mix crumbs and parmesan cheese.

Dip shrimp in egg mixture, roll in crumbs and fry in hot oil.

Golden Mushroom Chops

Contributed by Phil himsel'ph!

Ingredients:

- **4-6 pork chops**
- **1 can Campbell's Golden Mushroom soup**
- **Onions**
- **8 oz. milk**

Directions:

Cook and season chops as desired.

Pour soup, milk and sliced onions in pan and stir.

Simmer for 20-30 minutes.

Serve over mashed potatoes.

Cook's Tip!

To keep potatoes from budding, place an apple in the bag with the potatoes being stored.

Parmesan Chicken

Contributed by Katie Staige
(Phil and Karen's daughter)

Ingredients:

- **Boneless/skinless chicken breasts**
- **Bread crumbs (I like to use seasoned croutons)**
- **Nature's Seasoning**
- **Parmesan cheese**

Directions:

Preheat oven to 325 degrees.

Mix bread crumbs and Nature's Seasoning into a bowl.

Melt butter in a separate bowl.

Cut chicken into strips and roll in butter, then roll in breading and then place in appropriate baking pan.

Bake 30-40 minutes.

Sweet Mongolian Chicken

Contributed by Susan Carter

Ingredients:

- **1/2 cup soy sauce**
- **1/2 cup water**
- **3/4 cup brown sugar**
- **1/4 tsp. ginger powder**
- **1/2 Tbsp. garlic powder**
- **3 Tbsp. cornstarch mixed with 1/4 cup cold water**

- **2 cups cooked, cut up chicken**
- **2 cups broccoli, cooked and drained**
- **2 large green onions, diced**

- **Cooked white or brown rice**

Directions:

Combine soy sauce and water in large frying pan over medium heat. Add brown sugar and dissolve, stirring constantly. Stir in ginger and garlic. Bring to boil and slowly stir in cornstarch-water mixture, cook until thickened, about one minute.

Stir in chicken and broccoli, and cook until heated through.

Remove from heat, add green onions, and serve over rice.

Baked Almond Chicken

Contributed by Jim Grupa
Adapted from Taste of Home 2000

Ingredients:

- **½ cup all-purpose flour**
- **1/3 cup plus 1 Tbsp. butter or margarine, melted, divided**
- **1 tsp. celery salt**
- **1 tsp. paprika**
- **½ tsp. salt**
- **½ tsp. curry powder**
- **½ tsp. dried oregano**
- **¼ tsp. pepper**
- **6 boneless chicken breasts**
- **1 ½ cups whipping cream**
- **1/3 cup dry bread crumbs**
- **¾ cup sliced almonds, toasted**
- **Hot cooked pasta**

Directions:

Place flour in a shallow bowl. Combine 1/3 cup butter and seasonings in another bowl. Coat chicken with flour, then dip in butter mixture. Arrange in a greased shallow 3-quart baking dish. Pour cream around chicken.

Bake, uncovered, at 350 degrees for 45 minutes.

Combine bread crumbs and remaining butter; sprinkle over chicken. Top with almonds.

Bake, uncovered, for 5-8 minutes or until golden brown.

Serve over pasta.

Beefy Hash Brown Pizza

Contributed by Jim Grupa
Adapted from Taste of Home 2003 Annual Recipes

Ingredients:

- **5 cups frozen shredded hash brown potatoes, thawed**
- **1 can (10 3/4 ounces) cheddar cheese soup, undiluted**
- **1 egg, lightly beaten**
- **1/2 teaspoon salt**
- **1/4 teaspoon pepper**
- **2 pounds ground beef**
- **1 medium onion, chopped**
- **1 can (4 ounces) mushroom stems and pieces, drained**
- **1 can (15 ounces) pizza sauce**
- **4 cups (16 ounces) shredded pizza cheese, divided**

Directions:

In a bowl, combine the potatoes, soup, egg, salt and pepper. Spread mixture into a greased 15-in. x 10-in. x 1-in. baking pan. Bake at 400 deg. for 20-25 minutes or until lightly browned.

Meanwhile, in a large skillet over medium heat, cook the beef, onion and mushrooms until meat is no longer pink; drain. Stir in pizza sauce; keep warm. Sprinkle 2 cups cheese over hot crust. Spread meat mixture over the top; sprinkle with remaining cheese. Bake 5-10 minutes longer or until cheese is melted. Yield: 6-8 servings.

Bob Evans Sausage Gravy and Biscuits

Contributed by Jim Grupa
Source: CopyKat.com

Ingredients:

- **2 ½ cups Bisquick baking mix**
- **1 tsp. baking powder**
- **1 1/3 cups buttermilk (use a little more if needed)**
- **1 lb. extra mild breakfast sausage (Owens)**
- **6 Tbsp. flour**
- **1 ½ cups water**
- **2 ¼ cups whole milk (more if gravy is too thick)**
- **¾ tsp. salt**
- **1 tsp. paprika**

Directions:

Biscuits: Mix Bisquick, baking powder, and buttermilk until blended. On a floured board knead dough about ten times, until dough is easy to roll out, but not dry. Roll to ½" thickness, cut rounds 2 ½" in diameter. Bake 8 - 12 minutes or until done.

Gravy: On medium heat crumble and brown sausage in fry pan, stirring often. Remove sausage. Mix pan drippings with vegetable oil to measure ¼ cup. Cook on medium low heat and add flour one tablespoon at a time, whisking constantly until flour thickens and turns light brown. Slowly add water and stir. When flour mixture is smooth add milk, paprika, and salt. Stir until blended. Simmer, but do not boil. When blended add sausage, mix and simmer until heated through.

Cook's Tip!

When you cut out biscuits from the dough, press the flour-dipped cutter straight down - do not twist! Twisting seals edges of the biscuits and they won't rise as high.

Quick Spaghetti Sauce

Contributed by Carol Saecker

Ingredients:

- **1 lb. ground beef**
- **1 onion, chopped**
- **2 cloves garlic, minced**
- **Two 8 oz. cans tomato sauce**
- **6 oz. can tomato paste**
- **2 tsp. instant coffee**
- **Two 4 oz. cans mushrooms, reserve 2/3 cup liquid**
- **1 Tbsp. sugar**
- **1 Tbsp. Italian seasonings**

Directions:

Brown ground beef, onion and garlic; drain. Add tomato sauce and paste. Mix reserved liquid and instant coffee then add to ground beef mixture. Add mushrooms, sugar and seasoning.

Simmer 30 minutes and serve over hot cooked pasta.

Pork Chops with Mushroom Gravy

Contributed by Martha Baxter

Ingredients:

- **8 pork chops**
- **1 can Cream of Mushroom soup, condensed**
- **1/2 can milk**
- **1/2 medium onion, sliced**
- **2 Tbsp. canola oil**
- **1 tsp. salt**
- **1/2 tsp. pepper**
- **1/2 tsp. garlic powder**
- **1 tsp. beau monde seasoning (Spice Islands)**

Directions:

Heat the oil over medium heat in a large skillet (not non-stick, if possible). Blend the spices and season the pork chops with the spices on both sides. Brown the pork chops in the hot oil. Remove the chops. Add the mushroom soup and the milk to the skillet and blend until smooth, scraping the brown particles from the bottom of the pan. Add sliced onions and mix with soup. Add the chops, spoon the onion-soup mixture over the chops, cover, and cook for 1 hour over low heat. Goes great with garlic mashed potatoes.

Cook's Tip!

If your gravy begins to separate, add a pinch or two of baking soda to emulsify the fat in a matter of seconds.

Phil's Ph'amous Baby Back Ribs

Contributed by Phil himsel'ph!

Ingredients:

- **Baby back ribs**
- **Wye River Red Seasoning (Phil's ph'avorite)**
- **Wye River Black Seasoning (Phil's ph'avorite)**
- **Option - your ph'avorite seasonings**

Directions:

Heat grill (preferred smoking bits of a fruit wood). Once smoking good - reduce heat to 250 degrees.

Season ribs with favorite seasoning(s).

Grill for 4 hours, indirect heat if possible. Enjoy!

Blackened Spice

Contributed by Karen Staige
(Phil's wi'phe)

Ingredients:

- **Your choice of chicken, beef or fish**

Mix together:
- **1 Tbsp. paprika**
- **2 1/2 tsp. salt**
- **1 tsp. onion powder**
- **1 1/2 tsp. garlic powder**
- **1/2 tsp. thyme**
- **1/2 tsp. whole oregano**
- **1 tsp. white pepper**
- **1 tsp. black pepper**
- **1/2 tsp. cayenne pepper**

Directions:

Heat pan (cast iron recommended) on stove or grill on high heat. Pan is hot enough when a drop of butter instantly sizzles.

Cut desired meat to any size you like. Our favorite is boneless/skinless chicken breasts cut into strips (bone in chicken, steaks and fish work well also).

Roll meat in melted butter, then roll in blackened spice mixture and then carefully place into HOT pan and cook until done or, for chicken, until juices run clear.

Enchiladas de Pollo

Contributed by Janet Stanton (Phil's sister)

Ingredients:

- **2 whole chicken breasts**
- **Water**
- **1/2 small onion**
- **1 bay leaf**
- **8 peppercorns**
- **Salt**
- **1/2 medium onion, chopped**
- **3 Tbsp. grated Parmesan cheese**
- **4 oz. Monterey Jack cheese, shredded (1 cup)**
- **1 (4-oz.) can green chiles**
- **1 (13-oz.) can tomatillos, drained or 1-3/4 cups drained canned tomatoes**
- **1/4 cup cilantro leaves**
- **3/4 cup whipping cream**
- **1 egg**
- **Salt**
- **8 flour tortillas**
- **4 oz. cheddar or Monterey Jack cheese, shredded (1 cup)**
- **Guacamole (recipe follows)**
- **1 cup dairy sour cream**
- **3 or 4 radishes, sliced**
- **2 cups shredded lettuce**
- **12 ripe olives**

Directions:

Place chicken breasts in a large pot or Dutch oven. Add water to cover, onion, bay leaf, peppercorns and salt to taste. Bring to a boil; reduce heat. Cover and simmer 45

Pork Roast with Cranberry Glaze

Contributed by Janet Stanton (Phil's sister)

Ingredients:

- **3 Tbsp. cornstarch**
- **1/4 tsp. cinnamon**
- **1/8 tsp. salt**
- **6 Tbsp. orange juice (fresh squeezed preferred)**
- **1 (16-oz.) can whole cranberry sauce**
- **1 (3 to 5 lb.) boneless pork loin**

Directions:

Preheat over to 325 degrees.

In small saucepan, combine cornstarch, cinnamon and salt. Stir in orange juice and cranberry sauce. Cook over medium heat, stirring, until thickened and set aside.

Place pork in a shallow roasting pan and cover with about half the cranberry mixture. Insert a meat thermometer. Roast 1 to 1 1/2 hours, basting occasionally with the remaining sauce. Meat is done when thermometer reads 160 degrees F.

Remove meat from oven and allow to rest 10 minutes before carving.

Roasted Mediterranean Chicken

Contributed by Janet Stanton (Phil's sister)

Ingredients:

- **1-1/4 cups Healthy Choice Four Cheese Alfredo Sauce or any Alfredo sauce you like**
- **4 tsp. fresh lemon juice**
- **1 Tbsp. olive oil**
- **1/2 tsp. black pepper**
- **1/4 tsp. salt**
- **5 garlic cloves, crushed**
- **4 (4 oz.) skinless/boneless chicken breast halves**
- **cooking spray**
- **8 small red potatoes (about 1 lb.)**
- **8 plum tomatoes, quartered**
- **1 (14 oz.) can artichoke hearts, drained**
- **10 garlic cloves, peeled**
- **1 Tbsp. chopped fresh or 1 tsp. dried rosemary**
- **12 large pitted ripe olives, quartered**
- **Rosemary sprigs (optional)**

Directions:

Preheat oven to 450 degrees.

Combine first 6 ingredients. Arrange chicken in a 13x9 inch baking dish coated with cooking spray. Brush 3/4 cup sauce mixture over chicken. Arrange potatoes, tomatoes, artichokes, and 10 garlic cloves around chicken. Brush vegetables with 1/3 cup sauce mixture. Sprinkle with chopped rosemary and olives.

Bake at 450 degrees for 20 minutes. Brush chicken and vegetables with remaining sauce mixture, bake an additional 25 minutes or until potatoes are tender. Garnish with rosemary sprigs, if desired. 4 servings.

Henrietta's Chow Mein

Contributed by Ann Watkowski

Ingredients:

- **1 lb. chow mein meat**
- **3 Tbsp. soy sauce**
- **3 stalks celery, diced**
- **1 cup chopped onion**
- **1 can undrained Chinese vegetables**
- **1 can undrained mushrooms**
- **4 Tbsp. molasses**
- **3 Tbsp. soy sauce**
- **2 cups water**

Directions:

Brown meat, add soy sauce. Combine with remaining ingredients and simmer 2 hours.

Before serving, mix 2 tablespoons corn starch with a little water and stir into chow mein to thicken.

Serve with rice.

Spicy Chicken Legs

Contributed by Christina Staige

Ingredients:

- **2 Tbsp. canola oil**
- **2 tsp. paprika**
- **1 tsp. dried thyme**
- **1 tsp. chili powder**
- **½ tsp. dried cumin**
- **½ tsp. garlic powder**
- **½ tsp. salt**
- **½ tsp. pepper**
- **¼ tsp. ground nutmeg**
- **6 chicken legs with thighs, rinsed and patted dry**

Directions:

In a small bowl, mix oil and spices. Rub chicken legs with spice mixture and arrange on a baking sheet. Refrigerate 30 minutes.

Heat oven to 350 degrees. Bake chicken 40-45 minutes or until cooked through.

Also very good cooked on the grill.

Tator Tot Hot Dish

Contributed by Allen Staige

Ingredients:

- **2 lbs. lean hamburger**
- **1 small onion, chopped**
- **1 pkg. frozen corn**
- **1 can Cream of Mushroom soup (can use 2 cans)**
- **1 32 oz. pkg. frozen tator tots**

Directions:

Heat oven to 350 degrees. Wash hands!

Brown hamburger in pan with onion. Be sure to drain.

Stir in corn and soup.

Pour into whatever sized pan will hold it.

Top it with tots.

Bake for 45 minutes.

Serves 2 hungry people!

Chicken Casserole

Contributed by Joan Staige

Ingredients:

- **3-4 cups cooked chicken, diced**
- **2 cans Cream of Mushroom soup**
- **1 small onion, diced**
- **1 & ½ cups chicken broth**
- **1 cup milk**
- **½ lb. of Velveeta or cheddar cheese**
- **Diced green pepper (optional)**
- **Sliced mushrooms (optional)**

Directions:

Combine all in a large bowl. When mixed thoroughly pour into a greased 9 x 13 inch cake pan. Place in refrigerator overnight.

Top with buttered bread crumbs. Bake at 350 degrees for 1 hour, uncovered. (Bake longer if not heated through.)

Grandma Joanie's Meatballs and Noodles

Contributed by Amanda & Brooklyn Staige

Ingredients:

- **1 lb. ground beef**
- **1 small onion, chopped fine**
- **1 tsp. salt**
- **¼ tsp. thyme**
- **½ cup dry bread crumbs**
- **1 egg, slightly beaten**
- **1 can tomato soup**
- **1/3 cup water**
- **1 Tbsp. butter, melted**
- **1 6 oz. pkg. noodles, cooked**

Directions:

Mix beef, onion, salt, thyme, bread crumbs and egg together. Form into 6 large or 12 small balls.

Combine soup and water, heat to boiling point.

Drop meat balls into soup, cover and let simmer about 50 minutes.

Add butter to the noodles and serve with meat balls.

Mashed Potatoes and Hamburger Gravy

Contributed by Christapher Staige

Ingredients:

- **2 lbs. hamburger**
- **1 envelope Lipton Onion Soup**
- **2 cans Cream of Mushroom soup**
- **1 can milk**
- **Boiled, mashed potatoes**
- **1 can potato water (save after spuds are done!)**

Directions:

Brown the hamburger. Drain off grease. Add the onion soup mix and the 2 cans of mushroom soup, one can of milk and 1 cup of the potato liquid. Heat through, adding more potato water if necessary to make the consistency of gravy. Salt and pepper to taste.

Pour over mashed potatoes.

Cook's Tip!

To keep peeled potatoes white during cooking, add a small amount of white vinegar to the water.

Summertime Salmon

Contributed by Joan Staige

Ingredients:

- **2 Tbsp. soy sauce**
- **3 Tbsp. lemon juice or white wine**
- **¼ cup packed brown sugar**
- **½ tsp. ground ginger**
- **½ lb. salmon fillet (fresh)**

Directions:

Mix soy sauce, lemon juice or wine, brown sugar and the ginger in a shallow dish.

Add the salmon fillets, turn several times to coat.

Cover and refrigerate for an hour, turning once.

Foil the rack on the grill. Place salmon skin side down on the foil. Do not turn fillet during cooking. Salmon is done when it flakes easily.

Very, very good!

Party Chicken

This is so simple and so good!

Contributed by Pat Staige (Phil's sister)

Ingredients:

- **Thinly sliced corned beef (packaged is fine)**
- **Bacon strips**
- **Boneless chicken breasts, halved**
- **1 can Cream of Mushroom soup**
- **10 ounces sour cream**
- **White pepper to taste**

Directions:

Line a medium sized casserole dish with corned beef.

Wrap a piece of bacon around each halved boneless chicken breast and place on the layer of corned beef.

Repeat this step for as long as it takes to make one layer of bacon wrapped chicken breasts on the corned beef.

Mix soup with sour cream and white pepper to taste. Pour this over the wrapped chicken breasts.

Bake uncovered at 350 degrees for 1 1/2 hours.

I sprinkle paprika and scallions on top for presentation.

For larger crowds, use bigger pan(s), and just add more soup and sour cream mixture.

Taa Daa!

Queso Flameado (Ph'laming Cheese)

Contributed by Bev Groteboer
(Ph'riend of Phil's sister, Janet Stanton)

Ingredients:

- **1 lb. pork sausage**
- **2 lbs. grated Marble Jack cheese**
- **1 bell pepper (thinly sliced)**
- **1 small onion (thinly sliced)**
- **Cilantro**
- **Cumin**
- **Lantana (Mexican Spice)**
- **Black pepper**
- **1 tsp. 151 Rum**
- **Flour tortillas (10)**

Directions:

Brown sausage then press grease out between paper towels — set aside.

In same skillet using non-stick spray, saute bell pepper and onions, Cilantro, Cumin, Lantana, and black pepper.

Add sausage back in towards the end just to reheat.

Put this in two cast iron fajita skillets or one large cast iron skillet and put into pre-heated oven on broil for 3 - 5 minutes (or until cheese is bubbling).

Remove from oven and splash the Rum on top and immediately light with a match. This will burn off in less than a minute.

Wrap small amount in flour tortillas adding salsa individually if desired. Makes 10.

Chicken Asparagus Casserole

Contributed by Joanie Staige

Ingredients:

- **2-3 cups cooked chicken (can use turkey or tuna)**
- **1 can asparagus**
- **1 cup American cheese, grated**
- **1 6 oz. pkg. noodles, cooked**
- **1 4 oz. can mushrooms & juice**
- **1 2 oz. jar pimento**
- **1 cup celery (diced very small)**
- **1/3 cup onion (diced very small)**
- **1/3 cup green pepper (diced very small)**
- **1 8 oz. water chestnuts, sliced (opt)**
- **1 can Cream of Mushroom soup**
- **1 can Cream of Chicken soup**
- **1/2 cup mayonnaise**

Directions:

Grease a 3-quart casserole. Layer noodles, chicken, asparagus, cheese, celery, mushrooms, onion, green pepper, water chestnuts.

Combine soups, mayo, and liquid from the mushrooms. Pour over the layered ingredients.

Cover and bake at 325 degrees for 1 hour.

Korean Style Short Ribs

Contributed by Susan Carter

Ingredients:

- **4 lbs. beef short ribs, 2 & 1/2 inches long**
- **½ cup soy sauce**
- **¼ cup water**
- **1 Tbsp. sugar**
- **1 Tbsp. sesame seeds, toasted (optional)**
- **1 tsp. tabasco pepper sauce (optional)**
- **½ tsp. garlic powder**

Directions:

Score meaty sides of ribs about ½ inch apart, and ½ inch deep both lengthwise and crosswise.

Combine remaining ingredients. Marinate ribs 2 hours or longer.

Grill or broil 4" from heat source for approximately 15 minutes or until brown and crisp.

Cook's Tip!

To add flavor to barbecued foods, place herbs on the hot coals.

Chicken and Mushroom Wellington

Contributed by Susan Carter

Ingredients:

- **1 17 & ¼ ounce pkg. frozen puff pastry sheets**
- **8 boneless chicken breast cutlets**
- **2 tsp. dried thyme leaves**
- **Salt and freshly ground pepper to taste**
- **5 Tbsp. butter**
- **1 onion, finely chopped**
- **¼ lb. fresh mushrooms, sliced**
- **2 Tbsp. parsley, chopped**
- **1 8-ounce package cream cheese**
- **2 Tbsp. Dijon mustard**
- **One egg, beaten slightly with 2 Tbsp. water**

Directions:

Thaw pastry 20 minutes.

Sprinkle chicken with seasonings. In a medium skillet, brown chicken in 3 tablespoons butter; set aside. Add remaining butter to skillet, add onion and mushrooms, sauté until tender and liquid has evaporated. Stir in parsley.

On a lightly floured surface, roll each sheet of pastry to 14" square and cut into 4 7-inch squares to make 8 squares.

Preheat oven to 375 degrees.

Combine cream cheese and mustard, spread over chicken cutlets. Spread each pastry square with 2 tablespoons of the mushroom-onion mixture. Place chicken breast on top. Brush edges of pastry with water and wrap pastry around chicken. Press edges together to seal. Place seam side down on ungreased baking sheet and brush tops with egg-water mixture.

Bake 25 minutes or until puffed and golden brown.

Slow Cooked Sesame Chicken

Contributed by Nick and Lori Edstrom

Ingredients:

- **1 frying chicken, cut up**
- **3 Tbsp. sesame seeds**
- **¼ tsp. pepper**
- **1 small onion, chopped**
- **½ cup dry white wine**
- **½ tsp. tarragon**
- **¼ cup water**
- **¼ cup flour**
- **½ tsp. salt**
- **¼ cup salad oil**
- **2 stalks celery, chopped**
- **1 chicken bouillon cube, crumbled**
- **¼ cup cornstarch**
- **1 cup dairy sour cream**

Directions:

Coat chicken with mixture of flour, sesame seeds, salt and pepper. Heat oil in large skillet and brown chicken. Add onion, celery, wine, bouillon cube and tarragon. Cover and cook on low 6-8 hours.

Turn control to high and remove chicken to warm dish.

Dissolve cornstarch in water, and stir into remaining liquid in skillet. Cook on high 15 minutes. Turn heat off and stir in sour cream.

Pour sauce over chicken and serve with rice.

Note: This recipe can also be made in a crockpot.

Ph'ried Rice with Shrimp

Contributed by Nick and Lori Edstrom

Ingredients:

- **½ cup brown rice**
- **½ cup wild rice**
- **2 & ½ cups boiling water with 1 teaspoon salt or 1 Tbsp. soy sauce**
- **½ lb. fresh snow peas**
- **½ lb. fresh shrimp, chopped**
- **½ lb. fresh mushrooms, chopped**
- **2 Tbsp. butter**

Directions:

Combine brown and wild rice and cook in boiling water until light and fluffy (for timing, refer to cooking directions on package).

Saute the shrimp, mushrooms and snow peas in butter. Add hot rice and stir together for 1 minute. Serve immediately.

Chicken Lasagna

Contributed by Kathy Sheridan
(Ph'riend of a ph'riend)

Ingredients:

- **3 cups chicken (cooked, boneless, skinless breasts)**
- **1 pkg. lasagna (cooked)**
- **2 cans evaporated milk (14 1/2 oz. each)**
- **2 pkgs. dry Ranch dressing mix**
- **2 cups mozzarella cheese**
- **2 cups cheddar cheese**

Directions:

Stir Ranch dressing mix into evaporated milk and heat on stove until mixture thickens. Add chicken.

In a 9x13 inch pan, layer noodles, chicken, sauce and cheese. Repeat layers until your run out. Bake at 350 degrees until cheese is melted and it's hot throughout.

Variation: Add to sauce (before baking) a combination of broccoli, mushrooms, asparagus, and ricotta cheese.

Smothered Burritos

Contributed by Lynn Johnson & "Big Jer"
(Phil's cousin)

Ingredients:

- **1 pack of flour tortillas**
- **1 lb. hamburger, browned**
- **1 10-ounce can tomato paste, plus 3 cans of water**
- **1 package taco seasoning**
- **6 ounces shredded cheddar cheese**

Directions:

Mix hamburger, tomato paste and seasoning together. Put some of the mixture in each tortilla and roll up. Pour remaining sauce over all and sprinkle with cheese.

Bake at 350 degrees for 20-30 minutes.

Cook's Tip!

Leftover sauce? Spray your plastic containers with nonstick cooking spray before pouring in tomato-based sauces and there won't be any stains.

Auntie Do Do's Chicken Ala King

Contributed by Lynn Johnson & "Big Jer"
(Phil's cousin)

Ingredients:

- **½ cup butter**
- **½ cup flour**
- **1 tsp. salt**
- **¼ tsp. pepper**
- **1 ¾ cups chicken broth**
- **2 cups milk (mocha mix or your favorite half-and-half, or milk substitute)**
- **2 cups cooked chicken, chopped**
- **1 can mushrooms**
- **1 small can pimentos, drained**

Directions:

Melt butter, then mix in flour, salt, pepper, broth and milk. Stir until thickened.

Add chicken, mushrooms, and pimentos.

Serve over mashed potatoes, toast or biscuits.

Auntie Do Do's Ham Buns

Contributed by Lynn Johnson & "Big Jer"
(Phil's cousin)

Ingredients:

- **½ lb. ham**
- **2 green peppers**
- **1 pint stuffed green olives, drained**
- **2 Tbsp. minced onion**
- **1 lb. American cheese, shredded**
- **1 8-ounce can tomato sauce**

Directions:

Put all ingredients – except tomato sauce – through meat grinder. Add sauce to the ground up mixture. Fill ham buns, wrap in foil, and bake at 350 degrees for 15-20 minutes.

This will make 30 buns – great for a party.

Auntie Do Do's Chow Mein (crock pot version)

Contributed by Lynn Johnson & "Big Jer"
(Phil's cousin)

Ingredients:

- **1 lb. chow mein meat, browned**
- **1 stalk celery, including leaves**
- **1 onion**
- **1 15-ounce can Chinese vegetables**
- **3 Tbsp. molasses**
- **4 Tbsp. soy sauce**
- **Salt and pepper to taste**

Directions:

Combine all ingredients in a crock pot. Cook about 6-8 hours on high. Take out what you'll eat for dinner. Bring to simmer. Thicken with a water-cornstarch mixture.

Serve with chow mein noodles and rice.

Freeze leftovers.

Cook's Tip!

Celery can be kept in the freezer until needed for cooking. Chop into bite-sized pieces and put into plastic freezer bags in 1-cup servings.

Chow Mein Hot Dish

Contributed by Lynn Johnson & "Big Jer"
(Phil's cousin)

Ingredients:

- **1 lb. hamburger**
- **2 onions**
- **1 cup celery, chopped**
- **½ cup uncooked rice**
- **1 can Cream of Chicken soup**
- **1 can Cream of Mushroom soup**
- **1 can peas, undrained**
- **1 cup water**
- **4 Tbsp. soy sauce**

Directions:

Brown hamburger, onions, and celery. Drain. Combine all ingredients in a covered casserole and bake at 325 degrees for 2 hours.

Apricot Dijon Chicken

Contributed by Lynn Johnson & "Big Jer"
(Phil's cousin)

Ingredients:

- **1 ½ cups apricot nectar**
- **3 Tbsp. Dijon mustard**
- **Diced apricots**
- **Chicken breasts**

Directions:

Bring nectar, mustard and apricots to boil. Add chicken breast and cook until done, about 20 minutes, covered.

Chow Mein Noodle Hot Dish

Contributed by Jody Boughton
(Phil's cousin)

Ingredients:

- **Small bag chow mein noodles**
- **Chopped turkey or chicken**
- **1 cup onion, chopped**
- **2 celery, chopped**
- **Cashews**
- **1 can Cream of Mushroom soup**
- **1 can Cream of Chicken soup**
- **1 cup milk**

Directions:

Layer in a 9 x 13 inch pan: ½ bag noodles, turkey, onions, celery and cashews.

Combine soups and milk, pour on top. Sprinkle remaining noodles on top.

Bake in 350 degree oven for 1 hour.

Cook's Tip!

Wrap celery in aluminum foil when putting in the refrigerator and it will keep for weeks.

(Crockpot) Hamburger Casserole

Contributed by Jody Boughton
(Phil's cousin)

Ingredients:

- **2 large potatoes, sliced**
- **2-3 medium carrots, sliced**
- **1 #2 can peas, drained**
- **3 medium onions, sliced**
- **2 stalks celery, sliced**

- **1 ½ lbs. lean ground beef (or turkey), lightly browned**
- **1 10-ounce can tomato soup**
- **1 10-ounce can water**
- **Salt and pepper, to taste**

Directions:

Layer the vegetables in the order given into the crockpot. Season each layer with salt and pepper.

Place ground beef on top of the celery.

Mix the tomato soup with water and pour into crockpot.

Cover and set on low for 6-8 hours, or on high for 2-4 hours, stirring occasionally.

Crazy Crust Pizza

Contributed by Jody Boughton
(Phil's cousin)

Ingredients:

Batter:
- **1 cup flour**
- **1 tsp. salt**
- **1 tsp. oregano or Italian seasoning pepper**
- **2 eggs, slightly beaten**
- **2/3 cup milk**

Topping:
- **1 ½ lb. hamburger, browned; and/or 1 cup pepperoni**
- **¼ cup onions, chopped**
- **1 4-ounce can mushrooms, sliced**
- **1 cup pizza sauce (or substitute 8 ounces tomato sauce, 1-2 tsp. oregano and ¼ tsp. pepper)**
- **4 ounces mozzarella cheese**

Directions:

Preheat oven to 425 degrees. Lightly grease and flour a pizza pan.

Mix together batter ingredients and pour into pan. Arrange meat, onions, mushrooms, and any other of your favorite toppings on the batter. Bake on the lowest rack for 25-35 minutes or until brown. Remove from oven, drizzle with sauce and sprinkle with cheese. Bake additional 10-15 minutes.

Crisp Crab Cakes with Chardonnay Cream Sauce

Contributed by Susan Carter
Adapted from 1999 Bon Appetit

Ingredients:

- **1 3/4 cups Chardonnay or other dry white wine**
- **1/3 cup chopped shallots**
- **1 cup whipping cream**
- **1 1/2 lbs. crabmeat, drained (about 4 cups)**
- **2 1/2 cups finely crushed potato chips**
- **1 1/4 cups fresh breadcrumbs made from French bread**
- **1 7.25-ounce jar roasted red peppers, drained, coarsely chopped**
- **1/2 cup thinly sliced green onions**
- **2 large eggs**
- **2 Tbsp. chopped fresh dill**
- **1 Tbsp. Dijon mustard**
- **1 Tbsp. whole grain mustard**
- **1 Tbsp. mayonnaise**
- **1/4 cup (approximately) vegetable oil**

Directions:

Boil wine and shallots in heavy saucepan until mixture is reduced to 1/2 cup, about 10 minutes. Add cream and boil until sauce consistency, about 10 minutes. Season with salt and pepper.
Mix crabmeat, 1/2 cup crushed potato chips, breadcrumbs and next 7 ingredients in large bowl until well blended. Form into sixteen 2 1/2-inch diameter cakes. Place remaining potato chips in shallow dish. Press each cake into chips, turning to coat evenly.
Heat 2 tablespoons oil in heavy large skillet over medium-high heat. Working in batches, add crab cakes to skillet and cook until golden brown and heated through, adding more oil as necessary, about 5 minutes per side. Transfer crab cakes to paper-towel-lined plate to drain. Serve 2 crab cakes per plate topped with sauce.

Olive Garden Ph'ettuccine Alfredo

Contributed by Jim Grupa

Ingredients:

- **8 ounces cream cheese, cut in bits**
- **3/4 cup parmesan cheese, grated**
- **1/2 cup butter or margarine**
- **1/2 cup milk**
- **8 ounces fettuccine; cook and drain**

Directions:

In large saucepan combine cream cheese, parmesan, butter and milk, stirring constantly until smooth. Toss pasta lightly with sauce, coating well. Leftovers freeze well.

Cook's Tip!

Did you know you can freeze milk? Buy an extra carton and put it in the freezer. Defrost by simply placing in fridge overnight!

Chicken Tarragon En Croute

Contributed by Pam & Dan Callahan
(Ph'riends of a ph'riend, Doug MacLennan)

Ingredients:

- **2 chicken breasts (split, skinned, boned)**
- **1 (4 1/4-ounce) tube crescent roll dough**
- **1 egg (beaten)**
- **2 Tbsp. margarine**
- **1/2 tsp. lemon juice**
- **1/4 tsp. tarragon**
- **1/8 tsp. garlic salt**
- **1/8 tsp. black pepper**
- **Flour (for coating)**

Directions:

In small bowl, combine butter, lemon juice, tarragon, salt and pepper. Separate dough into two rectangles, press perfs to seal, roll each to 4" x 6".

Coat breasts in flour, place on each dough rectangle. Spread tarragon mixture evenly over each breast. Starting at shortest end, roll up jelly roll fashion, pinch ends/edges to seal. Place seam-side down on ungreased cookie sheet.

Cut slit in top of each bundle, bake at 375 degrees for 20 minutes. Brush with beaten egg and bake 5 minutes more.

Crab-Stuffed Chicken Breasts

Contributed by Pam & Dan Callahan
(Ph'riends of a ph'riend, Doug MacLennan)

Ingredients:

- **2 chicken breasts (split, skinned, boned)**
- **1/4 lb. crab meat (fresh or canned)**
- **1/4 lb. mushrooms (thinly sliced)**
- **1/2 cup shredded Swiss cheese**
- **1/2 cup chicken broth**
- **1/2 cup milk**
- **1/2 cup white wine**
- **1/4 cup green onion (thinly sliced)**
- **1/4 cup butter**
- **1/4 cup bread crumbs**
- **1/4 cup parsley**
- **3 Tbsp. flour**
- **1/4 tsp. thyme**

Directions:

Place breasts on cutting board between sheets of plastic. Flatten using a meat mallet until 1/4" thick.

Melt butter in large fry pan. Saute onions and mushrooms, blend in flour and thyme. Stir until bubbly. Slowly pour in broth, milk and wine. Heat, stirring until it boils and thickens. Add salt and pepper.

In small bowl, mix 1/4 cup each of: sauce, crab, parsley and crumbs. Divide mixture between breasts, fold edges up and over, and roll into bundles.

Place with seam side down in baking dish sprayed with vegetable oil. Spoon over remaining mixture and sprinkle with cheese. Bake covered at 375 degrees for 45 minutes.

Savory Stuffed Pork Chops

Contributed by Pam & Dan Callahan
(Ph'riends of a ph'riend, Doug MacLennan)

Ingredients:

- **2 pork chops (stuffed)**
- **1/2 cup dry red wine**
- **2 Tbsp. margarine**
- **1 Tbsp. lemon juice**
- **1/4 tsp. basil**
- **1/8 tsp. thyme**

Directions:

Spray baking dish with cooking oil. Pour in wine and lemon juice. Sprinkle in seasonings.

Add chops, place pad of margarine on each. Cover with foil, bake for 1-1/4 hour. Uncover, bake for 15 minutes to brown.

Portabella Mushroom Sandwiches with Tahini Sauce

Contributed by Susan Carter

Ingredients:

- **12 slices crusty whole wheat bread (crusty country bread or artisan-style rolls are especially good)**
- **1/4 cup vegetable oil**
- **4 large portabella mushrooms (about 1 1/4 pounds), stemmed, cut into 1/3-inch-thick slices**
- **1 large onion, thinly sliced**
- **2 tsp. Creole or Cajun seasoning**
- **2 tsp. lemon pepper seasoning**
- **2/3 cup purchased Ranch dressing**
- **1/4 cup tahini (sesame seed paste)**
- **1/4 cup milk**
- **12 thin tomato slices**
- **6 thin slices Swiss cheese**
- **Red leaf lettuce**

Directions:

Preheat broiler. Place bread in single layer on baking sheet. Broil until toasted.

Heat oil in heavy large skillet over medium-high heat. Add mushrooms and onion; sauté until tender, about 10 minutes. Add Creole seasoning and lemon pepper seasoning; sauté 2 minutes.

Whisk ranch dressing, tahini and milk in medium bowl to blend. Divide mushroom-onion mixture among 6 toasted bread slices. Top each with 1 tablespoon tahini sauce, 2 tomato slices, 1 slice Swiss cheese and lettuce. Top with second toasted bread slice and serve.

Meat Loaf Supreme

Contributed by Pam & Dan Callahan
(Ph'riends of a ph'riend, Doug MacLennan)

Ingredients:

- **1-1/2 lb ground beef**
- **1/2 lb ground pork**
- **1/4 cup onion (chopped)**
- **2 slices bacon**
- **1 large egg**
- **1 cup bread crumbs**
- **1/4 cup milk**
- **1/4 cup ketchup**
- **1/4 cup A-1 steak sauce**
- **1 Tbsp. horseradish**
- **1 Tbsp. parsley**
- **1 tsp. dry mustard**
- **1/2 tsp. salt**
- **1/2 tsp. thyme**
- **1/4 tsp. black pepper**

Directions:

Preheat oven to 350 degrees.

In mixing bowl, blend meat, onion and seasonings. In second bowl, blend eggs and milk. Add egg/milk mixture to meat bowl, mix in crumbs. Shape entire mixture into meat loaf pan. Top with bacon slices.

Bake for 50 minutes then remove.

Mix ketchup with A-1 sauce and pour over top.
Return to oven for 10 minutes.

Pheasant in Mushroom-Cream Sauce

Contributed by Pam & Dan Callahan
(Ph'riends of a ph'riend, Doug MacLennan)

Ingredients:

- **1 pheasant (skinned, cut up)**
- **2 Tbsp. olive oil**
- **2 Tbsp. margarine**
- **1 shallot (diced)**
- **2 cups wild mushroom (ideally morels)**
- **1/2 cup white wine**
- **1/2 cup chicken broth**
- **1 bay leaf**
- **1 cup cream (or half and half)**
- **2 Tbsp. dijon style mustard**
- **1 Tbsp. dill weed (or paprika)**

Directions:

Season meat with salt and pepper, brown over medium heat in olive oil and 1 tablespoon margarine. Remove meat, add 1 tablespoon margarine, saute mushrooms and shallots, saving 1/2 of juice.

Add wine, simmer briefly, then add broth and bay leaf. Bring to boil, return meat to pan and bake covered for 1 hour at 275 degrees.

Remove meat, discard bay leaf and place skillet over medium heat. Bring braising liquid to a boil, then stir in cream, allowing to thicken. Stir in mustard and dill, reduce heat to low, return meat to skillet until ready to serve.

Spoon sauce over meat and add a side dish of garlic mashed potatoes.

Asian Lettuce Wraps

Contributed by Jody Boughton
(Phil's cousin)

Ingredients:

- **¼ cup water**
- **1 Tbsp. cornstarch**
- **½ cup teriyaki sauce**
- **1-1¼ lb. boneless, skinless chicken breasts, thinly sliced**
- **1 can (8 ounces) whole water chestnuts, coarsely chopped**
- **2 Tbsp. vegetable oil**
- **Rice noodles**
- **Shredded carrots**
- **Iceberg lettuce leaves**

Directions:

Whisk together water and cornstarch in a large bowl until smooth. Stir in teriyaki sauce. Add chicken and water chestnuts; stir to coat. Marinate for 30 minutes.

Heat oil in wok or large skillet. Stir fry mixture until chicken is no longer pink. Place desired amount in lettuce leaves, top with rice noodles and shredded carrots. Roll up and enjoy!

Baked Ph'ish with Stuffing

Contributed by Jody Boughton
(Phil's cousin)

Ingredients:

- **4-6 fish fillets**
- **2 Tbsp. margarine**
- **1/3 cup broth**
- **½ cup onions, finely chopped**
- **½ cup carrots, shredded**
- **½ cup mushrooms, chopped**
- **¼ cup chopped parsley**
- **½ - ¾ cup bread crumbs**
- **1 beaten egg**
- **1 Tbsp. lemon juice**
- **1 tsp. salt**
- **1/8 tsp. pepper**

Directions:

Spray 9 x 13 inch pan with cooking spray. Place ½ of fish fillets in pan. Combine remaining ingredients and place on fillets. Top with another fillet (secure with toothpick if necessary), and sprinkle with paprika. Bake, uncovered, in 350 degree oven for ½ hour.

Pan-Ph'ried Walleye Ph'illets

Contributed by Pam & Dan Callahan
(Ph'riends of a ph'riend, Doug MacLennan)

Ingredients:

- **1-1/2 lb. walleye fillets**
- **1 egg (beaten)**
- **1/2 cup seasoned crouton crumbs**
- **1/4 cup parmesan cheese**
- **1/4 cup flour**
- **1 12-ounce can beer**
- **1 tsp. seasoning salt**
- **1 tsp. lemon pepper seasoning**

Directions:

In small bowl, mix flour and seasonings. In second bowl, mix egg and beer (or water). In third bowl, mix crumbs and cheese.

Rinse and dry fillets with paper towel. Dip fillets in the three bowls, in the order listed above. Heat oil in large fry pan. Fry fillets approximately five minutes per side. Garnish with lemon wedges.

Cook's Tip!

To easily remove burnt food on your skillet, add a drop of dish soap and enough water to cover bottom of pan, then bring to a boil on stovetop.

Pistachio-Crusted Chicken with Herbs & Cream Sauce

Contributed by Susan Carter

Ingredients:

- **1 cup shelled raw pistachios (about 4 ounces)**
- **1/2 cup panko (Japanese breadcrumbs)**
- **1/4 cup Dijon mustard**
- **2 Tbsp. chopped fresh basil**
- **1 Tbsp. chopped fresh dill**
- **1 tsp. chopped fresh rosemary**
- **4 5-ounce skinless boneless chicken breast halves**
- **2 Tbsp. (approximately) vegetable oil**
- **Mustard-Cream Sauce (recipe below)**

Directions:

Finely grind nuts in processor. Add panko and pulse to blend. Transfer to shallow baking dish. Mix mustard, basil, dill and rosemary in medium bowl. Spread mustard mixture over both sides of each chicken breast. Dip chicken breasts into nut mixture, coating completely. Sprinkle with salt and pepper. Heat 2 tablespoons oil in heavy skillet over medium heat. Saute 2 chicken breasts until golden brown, about 2 minutes per side. Transfer to baking sheet. Remove any leftover nuts from skillet; repeat with remaining chicken breasts. Bake chicken until cooked through, about 7 minutes. Spoon sauce over chicken and serve.

Cream Sauce:

- **1/2 cup dry white wine**
- **1/4 cup chopped shallots**
- **1 cup whipping cream**
- **2 Tbsp. Dijon mustard**
- **1 Tbsp. chopped fresh basil**
- **1 Tbsp. chopped fresh dill**

Boil wine and shallots in heavy saucepan over high heat until liquid evaporates, about 4 minutes. Reduce to medium-high. Add whipping cream, simmer about 2 minutes. Add mustard, basil and dill. Simmer 2 minutes to blend flavors. Season to taste with salt and pepper. Makes about 1 cup.

Sinful Desserts & "Sticky Ph'ingers" Sweets

Pumpkin Marble Cheesecake

A gingersnap cookie pecan crust and a swirl of pumpkin in every bite!

Contributed by Linda Grupa

Ingredients:

CRUST

- **2 ¼ cups gingersnap crumbs - break cookies into chunks with meat mallet, then use food processor to reduce to crumbs**
- **½ cup finely chopped pecans**
- **1/3 - ½ cup margarine or butter, melted**

FILLING

- **3 (8 oz.) pkgs. cream cheese, softened**
- **1 cup sugar, divided**
- **1 tsp. vanilla**
- **3 eggs**
- **1 cup canned pumpkin (or 15 oz. can (1 ½ cup)**
- **1 tsp. ground cinnamon**
- **¼ tsp. ground nutmeg**
- **Dash ground cloves**

Directions:

Mix crumbs, pecans and margarine; press onto bottom and 2-inches up sides of 9-inch pie pan. Bake 10 minutes in preheated 325 degree oven.

Beat cream cheese, ¾ cup sugar and vanilla at medium speed with electric mixer until well blended. Add eggs, 1 at a time, mixing at low speed after each addition, just until blended. Reserve 1 cup batter. Add remaining sugar, pumpkin and spices to remaining batter, mix well.

Spoon pumpkin and cream cheese batters alternately over crust; cut through batters with knife several times for marble effect. Bake 55-60 minutes or until center is almost set. Run knife or metal spatula around rim of pan to loosen cake; cool. Refrigerate 4 hours or overnight.

Steamed Cranberry Pudding

Contributed by Carol Saecker

Ingredients:

- **1 ½ cups flour**
- **2 cups fresh (or frozen) whole cranberries**
- **¼ cup sugar**
- **¼ tsp. salt**
- **2 tsp. baking soda**
- **1/3 cup hot water**
- **¼ cup unsulfured molasses**

Directions:

Sift together flour, sugar and salt. Rinse and pick over cranberries. Add to flour mixture and mix to coat berries. In separate bowl mix together the hot water and molasses, then mix in the baking soda. As you mix this it will begin to foam up. Once it does, add to the flour mixture and mix to combine. Place in separating angel food pan and suspend over boiling water in a large Dutch oven or steamer. Do not place the pan in the water, just over it to steam. Cover with aluminum foil. Steam for 1 hour to 1 ¼ hours. It is done when wooden pick inserted comes out clean. Cool completely and then remove from angel food pan. Slice into serving pieces and top with hot butter sauce.

Hot Butter Sauce:

- **½ cup butter**
- **1 cup sugar**
- **½ cup half & half**

In saucepan, melt butter then add sugar. Cook until sugar is melted (no longer "gritty"); add half & half and warm through.

Earthquake Cake

Contributed by Linda Grupa

Ingredients:

- **Cooking spray**
- **Coconut**
- **Pecans, chopped**
- **1 chocolate cake mix**
- **1 8 ounce cream cheese**
- **1 stick of butter or margarine**
- **2 cups powdered sugar**
- **Vanilla extract, to taste**

Directions:

Spray 9 X 13 inch pan with cooking spray.

Sprinkle a layer of coconut and a layer of chopped pecans on bottom of pan.

Prepare chocolate cake mix batter per directions and pour over coconut and pecans.

Mix cream cheese, butter, powdered sugar and vanilla until creamy. Spoon blobs of mixture on top of cake batter. Using a knife, swirl the mixture into the batter.

Bake at 350 degrees for 45 minutes to 1 hour. Let cool.

Caramel Cheesecake Squares

Contributed by Jim Grupa

Ingredients:

Crust:

- **2 cups flour**
- **1 cup butter**
- **½ cup brown sugar**
- **½ cup chopped nuts**

Filling:

- **28 caramels**
- **1 can sweetened condensed milk**

Topping: (beat with mixer)

- **2 (8-ounce each) packages cream cheese**
- **½ cup sugar**
- **3 eggs**
- **1 tsp. vanilla**

Directions:

Mix together crust ingredients and pat in bottom of a 9" x 13" greased pan. Save ¾ cup for topping.

Melt caramels in top of double-boiler or microwave. Pour melted caramels over crust.

In a mixer, beat topping ingredients, and layer on top of filling. Top with reserved crumbs.

Bake 35 minutes in 350 degree oven. When cool, refrigerate.

Cherry Pecan Dessert

Contributed by Becky Coltrain
(Ph'riend of a ph'riend)

Ingredients:

- **½ stick margarine**
- **2 cans cherry pie filling**
- **1 pkg. yellow cake mix**
- **1 stick margarine**
- **1 cup nuts**

Directions:

Melt ½ stick margarine 9 x 13 in pan. Spread pie filling in bottom. Sprinkle with dry cake mix.

Melt margarine and pour over cake mix. Sprinkle with nuts.

Bake at 350 degrees until golden brown 45 - 60 minutes.

(May also use apple.)

Cook's Tip!

If you're having trouble shelling nuts, putting them in the freezer for about an hour will make them easier to crack.

Sensational Peppermint Pattie Brownies

Contributed by Jane Palmer

Ingredients:

- **24 small (1 ½ inch) York peppermint patties**
- **1 ½ cups (3 sticks) butter or margarine, melted**
- **3 cups sugar**
- **1 Tbsp. vanilla**
- **5 eggs**
- **2 cups all-purpose flour**
- **1 cups Hershey's cocoa**
- **1 tsp. baking powder**
- **1 tsp. salt**

Directions:

Heat oven to 350 degrees (325 degrees for glass baking dish). Grease 13 x 9 inch baking pan.

Remove wrappers from peppermint patties.

Stir together butter, sugar and vanilla in large bowl. Add eggs; beat until well blended. Stir in flour, cocoa, baking powder and salt; blend well. Reserve 2 cups batter.

Spread remaining batter in prepared pan. Arrange peppermint patties about ½ inch apart in single layer over batter. Spread reserved 2 cups batter over patties.

Bake 50 to 55 minutes or until brownies begin to pull away from sides of pan. Cool completely in pan on wire rack; cut into squares.

Yields about 36 brownies.

Turtle Bars

Contributed by Sharon Woychek

Ingredients:

Bottom layer:
- **2 cups flour**
- **3/4 cup brown sugar**
- **1/2 cup butter**

Middle layer:
- **1 1/2 cups pecans**

Top layer:
- **1/2 cup brown sugar**
- **2/3 cup butter**

Topping:
- **1 & 1/2 cups milk chocolate chips**

Directions:

Mix bottom layer ingredients with a pastry blender until crumbly. Press into 9 x 13 inch pan.

Sprinkle pecans (middle layer) over crust.

Heat top layer ingredients, and stir until bubbly, plus another 30-60 seconds.

Pour over pecans.

Bake at 350 degrees 18-20 minutes until caramel bubbles and browns. Remove from oven.

Sprinkle chocolate chips on hot bars, let stand 3 minutes, then spread.

Rhubarb Whip Cream Cake

Contributed by Ann Speltz

Ingredients:

- **1 box yellow cake mix**
- **2 cups rhubarb (cleaned and cut into small pieces)**
- **1 cup sugar**
- **2 small containers whipping cream (do not whip)**

Directions:

Prepare cake mix as directed and pour batter into 9x13 inch baking pan. Spread rhubarb pieces over top of cake mix batter. Sprinkle sugar over top of rhubarb pieces. Pour unwhipped whipping cream over top.

Bake at 350 degrees for approximately 40 minutes.

Keep refrigerated.

Mint Cake

Contributed by Inez Miller
(Ph'riend of a ph'riend)

Ingredients:

- **1 package white cake mix**
- **1/4 - 1/2 cup creme de menthe, or mint flavoring, to taste**
- **1 jar hot fudge sauce**
- **Cool Whip topping**

Directions:

Prepare cake mix batter, and add creme de menthe or mint flavoring. Bake per directions.

When cake just comes out of oven, pierce top all over with meat fork or skewer.

Warm hot fudge sauce (in microwave) just long enough to make it of pouring consistency and pour sauce on top of cake.

Let cool.

Frost with Cool Whip mixed with a small amount of creme de menthe or mint flavor and color to taste.

Syllabub

Contributed by Inez Miller
(Ph'riend of a ph'riend)

Ingredients:

- **8 oz. white wine**
- **2 Tbsp. lemon juice**
- **1/4 cup grated rind of lemon**
- **1/4 cup sugar**
- **1/2 pint whipping cream**

Directions:

Put wine, sugar, lemon juice and rind in a bowl and let sit 3 hours. Overnight is best.

Add cream and whip until mixture stands in soft peaks.

Put in serving dishes and chill covered for several hours in refrigerator.

Serves 8.

Cook's Tip!

To get the most juice out of fresh lemons, bring them to room temperature and roll them under your palm against the kitchen counter before squeezing.

Quick Ph'ruit Cobbler

Contributed by Mary Wojciechowski
(Ph'riend of a ph'riend)

Ingredients:

- **1 can (21 ounces) fruit pie filling (any flavor)**
- **1 c. original Bisquick**
- **1/4 cup milk**
- **1 Tbsp. sugar**
- **I Tbsp. margarine or butter, softened**

Directions:

Spread pie filling in ungreased 1 1/2-quart casserole. Place in cold oven and turn oven to 400 degrees; let heat 10 minutes. Remove casserole from oven.

While pie filling is heating, stir remaining ingredients until soft dough forms.

Drop dough by 6 spoonfuls onto warm pie filling.

Sprinkled with additional sugar if desired.

Bake 18 to 20 minutes or until topping is golden brown.

Makes about 6 servings.

7 Layer Bars

Contributed by Jane Palmer

Ingredients:

Crust:
- **2 cups graham cracker crumbs**
- **¼ cup flour**
- **½ cup melted margarine**

Filling:
- **1 cup coconut**
- **6 oz. butterscotch chips**
- **6 oz. chocolate chips**
- **½ cup chopped nuts**

Topping:
- **1 can sweetened condensed milk**

Directions:

Mix crust ingredients and pat into 9 x 13 inch pan.

Mix filling ingredients and sprinkle over crust.

Pour condensed milk over all.

Bake at 350 degrees for 25 minutes.

Rice Krispies Treats

An old standard that never fails to satisfy!

Contributed by Mary Wojciechowski
(Ph'riend of a ph'riend)

Ingredients:

- **1 stick of margarine or butter**
- **1 package of miniature marshmallows**
- **6 cups of Rice Krispies or other rice cereal**

Directions:

Melt margarine in large saucepan over low heat. Add marshmallows and stir until completely melted. Remove from heat.

Add the rice krispies cereal. Stir until well coated.

Using buttered spatula or waxed paper, press mixture evenly into a 13 X 9 X 2 inch pan coated with cooking spray.

Yields about 24 squares.

Cook's Tip!

Store marshmallows in the freezer. To get them apart, cut with scissors that have been dipped in very hot water.

Rhubarb Goop

Contributed by Carol Saecker

Ingredients:

- **8 cups cut-up rhubarb, fresh or frozen**
- **1 cup brown sugar**
- **2 cups flour, sifted**
- **2 cups sugar**
- **4 tsp. baking powder**
- **1 tsp. salt**
- **2 eggs, beaten slightly**

Directions:

Spread cut-up rhubarb in bottom of 9 X 13 baking pan. Sprinkle brown sugar over top.

Mix together flour, sugar, baking powder, salt and eggs. Spread over rhubarb.

Bake at 350 degrees for 1 hour.

Serve warm with ice cream or whipped cream.

Blueberry Dream Dessert

Contributed by Jane Palmer

ingredients:

- **2 cups quick oats**
- **1 cup flour**
- **¾ cup melted margarine**
- **1 cup brown sugar**
- **1 can blueberry pie filling**

Directions:

Combine oats, flour, margarine and brown sugar. Save 1 cup for topping.

Spread crumbs in greased 8-inch square pan. Press firmly.

Spread pie filling over crumbs. Sprinkle with reserved crumbs.

Bake at 325 degrees for 35 minutes.

Yields 6 servings.

Banana Split

Contributed by Jane Palmer

Ingredients:

- **½ cup butter, melted**
- **2 cups graham cracker crumbs**
- **2 eggs**
- **2 cups sifted powdered sugar**
- **¾ cup butter softened**
- **1 tsp. vanilla**
- **1 (20 oz.) can crushed pineapple, well drained**
- **4 medium bananas (sliced) about 3 cups**
- **1 (9 oz.) carton Cool Whip**
- **½ cup coarse ground pecans**
- **1 (4 oz.) jar maraschino cherries**

Directions:

Combine butter and crumbs. Pat into bottom of 13 x 9 inch pan.

Beat eggs at high speed for 4 minutes. Add powdered sugar, softened butter and vanilla. Beat 5 minutes. Spread over crumbs. Chill 30 minutes.

Spread pineapple over creamed mixture.

Arrange bananas over pineapple.

Cover with Cool Whip.

Sprinkle with pecans.

Cover and refrigerate 6 hours. Garnish with cherries.

Old-Fashioned White Cookies

Contributed by Ann Watkowski
(Ph'riend of a ph'riend)

Ingredients:

Mix in order:

- **2 cups sugar**
- **1/2 cup butter**
- **1/2 cup shortening**
- **2 eggs, beaten**
- **1 cup sour milk mixed with 1 tsp. soda**
- **1/4 tsp. salt**
- **1 tsp. nutmeg**
- **4 cups flour**

Chill, roll out and cut out with large mouthed glass.

Place on cookie sheet and bake at 350 degrees about 10 minutes or until edges are very lightly browned.

Cook's Tip!

Instead of dipping cookie cutters in flour, dip in water. Dough drops right off the cutter with no mess!

Pumpkin Torte

Contributed by Rose Mary Staige

Ingredients:

Crust:

- **20 graham crackers (crushed)**
- **½ cup melted butter**
- **2 eggs, beaten**
- **¾ cup sugar**
- **8 oz. cream cheese**

Filling:

- **2 cups canned pumpkin**
- **3 egg yolks**
- **½ cup sugar**
- **½ cup milk**
- **½ tsp. salt**
- **1 tsp. each cinnamon and allspice**
- **1 envelope plain gelatin dissolved in ¼ cup cold water**
- **3 egg whites**
- **¼ cup sugar**

Directions:

Mix graham crackers and butter, press into a buttered 9 x 13 inch pan.

Beat eggs, sugar and cream cheese, pour over crust and bake 20 minutes at 350 degrees. Cool. Combine pumpkin, egg yolks, sugar, milk, salt, cinnamon and allspice, cook and stir until thickened. Add gelatin mix.

Beat egg whites, then add ¼ cup sugar and continue to beat until fluffy. Fold into pumpkin mixture and pour over cooled crust. Refrigerate. Decorate with whipped cream.

Special "K" Bars

Contributed Rose Mary Staige

Ingredients:

- **½ cup white sugar**
- **½ cup white syrup**
- **¾ cup peanut butter**
- **3 cups Special K cereal**
- **½ pkg. butterscotch chips**
- **1 pkg. milk chocolate chips**
- **¼ cup milk**

Directions:

Combine sugar and syrup and bring just to boiling, but do not boil. Remove from stove.

Add peanut butter and cereal. Pat into a 9" x 13" buttered pan.

Melt butterscotch chips and chocolate chips in milk. Frost over top & cool.

Chocolate Caramel Bars

Contributed by Rose Mary Staige

Ingredients:

- **1 pkg. German chocolate cake mix**
- **1/3 cup evaporated milk (1/2 of a 5 oz. can)**
- **½ cup softened butter**

- **40 caramels**
- **¼ cup butter**
- **1/3 cup evaporated milk**

- **1 cup semi-sweet chocolate chips (optional)**
- **1 cup chopped nuts (optional)**

Directions:

Heat oven to 350 degrees.

Mix cake mix, 1/3 cup evaporated milk and softened butter until crumbly. Press ½ of this cake mixture into a greased 9" x 13" pan. Bake at 350 degrees for 6 minutes.

Melt caramels, ¼ cup butter and 1/3 cup evaporated milk in microwave until caramels are completed melted, stirring occasionally. Pour over baked cake mixture; sprinkle with chocolate chips and chopped nuts, and top with reserved cake mixture.

Bake 15 to 18 minutes at 350 degrees.

Rhubarb Cake

Contributed by Joan Staige

Ingredients:

- **1 pkg. yellow cake mix**
- **4 cups chopped fresh or frozen rhubarb**
- **1 cup sugar**
- **1 cup whipping cream**

Directions:

Prepare cake batter according to package directions. Pour into a greased 13x9 inch cake pan. Sprinkle with rhubarb and sugar. Slowly pour cream over the top.

Bake 350 degrees for 40-45 minutes or until done. Cool.

Can invert pan onto a serving tray so the rhubarb will be on top, or serve from the pan. Serve with whipped cream or cool whip.

Cook's Tip!

When using cake mixes, put the water in the bowl BEFORE putting in the dry mix to prevent dry pockets of powder on the bottom of the bowl after you've mixed the cake.

Salted Nut Bars

Contributed by Jane Palmer

Ingredients:

- **24 oz. salted peanuts, divided**
- **1 pkg. Reese's peanut butter chips**
- **1 stick margarine**
- **1 can sweetened condensed milk**
- **1 (10 ½ oz.) bag miniature marshmallows**

Directions:

Butter a 9 x 13 inch pan and sprinkle with 12 ounces of peanuts.

Melt together peanut butter chips and margarine. Mix well.

Add sweetened condensed milk and stir well.

Stir in miniature marshmallows. Spread marshmallow mixture over top of peanut layer and then sprinkle top with remaining peanuts. Store in refrigerator.

Applesauce Cake

Contributed by Karen Staige
(Phil's wi'phe)

Ingredients:

- **2 cups unsweetened applesauce**
- **2 tsp. baking soda**
- **3/4 tsp. salt**
- **2 cups sugar**
- **1 cup shortening**
- **4 cups flour**
- **1 tsp. cinnamon**
- **Dash of nutmeg**
- **Dash of cloves**
- **1/2 lb. raisins**

Directions:

Preheat oven to 350 degrees.

Heat the unsweetened applesauce to almost a boil. Add baking soda and salt.

Mix together: sugar, shortening, flour, cinnamon, nutmeg, cloves and raisins.

Pour hot applesauce over top of mixture and mix well.

Pour into two (2) 3x5 bread pans (recommended) or a 9x13 inch pan, or two (2) 8 or 9 inch round cake pans.

Bake for 45 minutes.

Angel Gingerbread

Contributed by Karen Staige
(Phil's wi'phe)

Ingredients:

- **1 1/2 cups sugar**
- **3/4 cup butter**
- **3 eggs**
- **3/4 cup molasses**
- **3 cups flour (heaping)**
- **3/4 tsp. cinnamon**
- **1 1/2 cups boiling water**
- **3 tsp. baking soda (level)**

Directions:

Preheat oven to 325 degrees.

Cream sugar and butter.

Add eggs and beat well.

Add molasses.

Sift flour and cinnamon together into mixture.

Add soda to boiling water and add to mixture. Mix well.

Bake 1 hour.

Chocolate Bar Pie

Contributed by Florence Grupa

Ingredients:

- **Prepared graham cracker or chocolate cookie crust**
- **6 almond Hershey bars**
- **33 marshmallows**
- **½ cup milk**
- **1 pint whipping cream**

Directions:

Heat Hershey bars, marshmallows and milk in double boiler, mix, and set aside to cool.

Whip one pint of whipping cream, fold into cooled ingredients.

Spoon into prepared crust.

Set in refrigerator for 24 hours.

Cook's Tip!

Spray vegetable oil on your knife before cutting a pie with a cream filling to stop the filling from clinging to the knife.

Apple Pie Cake

Contributed by Florence Grupa

Ingredients:

- **1 cup white sugar**
- **½ cup butter or margarine**
- **1 egg**
- **1 tsp. baking soda dissolved in 2 Tbsp. hot water**
- **1 cup flour**
- **¼ tsp. nutmeg**
- **2-1/2 cups diced apple**
- **½ cup walnuts**
- **1 tsp. vanilla**

Directions:

Mix together sugar, butter, egg, baking soda mixture, flour and nutmeg.

Add apples, walnuts and vanilla.

Spoon batter into greased pan or pie tin.

Bake at 350 degrees for approximately 45 minutes or until toothpick inserted into the center comes out clean.

Butterfinger Candies

Contributed by Rose Mary Staige

Ingredients:

- **1 box Kraft Cheese Nips**
- **Peanut butter**
- **Chocolate almond bark (melted)**

Directions:

Frost Cheese Nips with peanut butter. Dip into melted almond bark and cool on waxed paper. (I recommend using a tweezers for the dipping process.)

Auntie Do Do's Bananas Frosting

Contributed by Lynn Johnson & "Big Jer"
(Phil's cousin)

Ingredients:

- **2 Tbsp. butter**
- **2 cups powdered sugar**
- **¼ tsp. salt**
- **1 tsp. vanilla**
- **½ medium banana**

Directions:

Beat together all ingredients until smooth and creamy.

This is awesome on angle food cake.

Cook's Tip!

To cut an angel food cake without squishing or smushing, use an electric knife or unwaxed dental floss.

Peanut Butter and Graham Cracker Toffee

Contributed by Susan Fryer
(Karen's sister)

Ingredients:

- **10 graham cracker sheets**
- **1/2 cup creamy peanut butter**
- **1 stick butter**
- **1 cup brown sugar**
- **1 cup semi-sweet chocolate chips**
- **1 cup pecans, chopped**

Directions:

Spread peanut butter on top of graham crackers.

Place graham, peanut butter side up on cookie sheet.

Bring butter and sugar to a boil in saucepan. Boil for 3 minutes, then spread over grahams.

Bake in preheated 350 degree oven for 3-4 minutes.

Sprinkle chocolate chips over grahams, wait for them to melt and spread evenly.

Sprinkle nuts over the top, freeze to set.

Bev's Very Best Chocolate Chip Cookies

Contributed by Bev Keiper

Ingredients:

- **2 cups butter**
- **2 cups of sugar**
- **2 cups brown sugar**
- **4 eggs**
- **2 tsp. vanilla**
- **4 cups of flour**
- **5 cups blended oatmeal***
  (I have also used a variety of flavored uncooked oatmeal cereal)
- **1 tsp. salt**
- **2 tsp. baking powder**
- **2 tsp. soda**
- **24-ounces chocolate chips**
- **1 8-ounce Hershey bar (grated)**
- **3 cups of nuts (your choice)**

Directions:

Cream the butter and both sugars.

Add eggs and vanilla: mix together with flour, oatmeal, salt, baking powder, and soda.

Add chocolate chips, grated Hershey bar, and nuts.
Roll into balls and place two inches apart on a cookie sheet.

Bake for 10 minutes at 375 degrees.

Makes 112 cookies.

* Measure oatmeal and blend in a blender to fine pieces.

Bev's Caramel-Cashew Bars

Contributed by Bev Keiper

Ingredients:

Crust

- **2 cups unbleached all purpose flour**
- **1 cup light brown sugar, packed**
- **4 ounces (1 stick) cold butter**
- **1 ½ cups cashew halves or pieces**

Caramel

- **¼ plus 3 Tbsp. butter (1 stick + 3 Tbsp.)**
- **½ cup light brown sugar, packed**

Directions:

Position oven rack in the center of the oven. Preheat oven to 350 degrees. Butter a 9 X 13" pan... I usually double recipe and put it in a cookie sheet.

To make crust, put flour & 1 cup brown sugar and butter in the large bowl. Mix on low until pea-size crumbs form. Press the crust firmly into the prepared pan. Sprinkle the cashews nuts evenly over the crust.

To make caramel, heat ¼ lb. butter plus 3 tablespoons and ½ cup of brown sugar in a medium saucepan. Cook over low-medium heat until the butter and brown sugar melt, stirring constantly.

Increase the heat to medium and bring to a boil for one minute, stirring constantly. Pour the hot mixture evenly over the cashews in the baking pan.

Bake until the mixture bubbles, about 25 minutes.

Makes 24 2-inch bars.

Oreo Truffles (Cookies & Cream Candy)

Contributed by Rose Mary Staige

Ingredients:

- **1 lb. 2 oz. pkg. Oreo cookies**
- **8 oz. cream cheese**
- **20 oz. vanilla almond bark (melted)**

Directions:

Crush Oreo cookies. Mix in cream cheese and roll into 1 inch balls.

Dip into melted Almond Bark until completed coated. (I recommend using a toothpick to dip balls.)

Place on sheet of waxed paper to cool.

Julie's Sugar Roll Outs

Contributed by Julie Bigaouette

Ingredients:

- **1 cup butter**
- **1 cup sugar**
- **2 eggs**
- **3 cups flour**
- **½ tsp. cream of tartar**
- **½ tsp. baking soda**
- **¼ tsp. salt**
- **1 tsp. vanilla**

Directions:

Cream butter and sugar together. Add eggs and mix well. Add flour, baking soda and cream of tart, salt and vanilla. Mix and chill for 1 hour.

Roll out dough and cut into shapes. Bake at 375 degrees for 10-12 minutes.

Note: I frost these with cream cheese frosting and decorate with "whatever" – yum-yum!

Cook's Tip!

To quickly frost batches of cookies, use a pastry brush instead of a knife to spread the frosting.

Chocolate Brownies

Contributed by Joan Staige

Ingredients:

Brownies:

- **1 cup sugar**
- **4 beaten eggs**
- **1 tsp. vanilla**
- **½ tsp. baking powder**
- **½ cup butter (do not substitute)**
- **1 16-ounce can Hershey's chocolate syrup**
- **1 cup flour**
- **½ cup nuts (optional)**

Frosting:

- **6 Tbsp. butter**
- **1 & ½ cups sugar**
- **6 Tbsp. milk**
- **¾ cup chocolate chips (Nestles are best)**

Directions:

Brownies: Beat together sugar, butter and eggs. Add can of syrup, vanilla, flour and baking powder. Mix well. Add nuts.

Bake in 9 x 13 pan for 25 minutes at preheated 350 degree oven.

Frosting: Boil butter, milk and sugar for 1 minute. Remove from heat and add chocolate chips. Beat well, until thick. Spread over bars.

Ph'rench Silk Pie

Contributed by Susan Carter

Ingredients:

- **1 sheet frozen pastry crust, thawed**
- **3 ounces unsweetened baking chocolate**
- **1 cup sugar**
- **¾ cup butter**
- **1 + ½ tsp. pure vanilla extract**
- **3 eggs**
- **1 cup cold heavy whipping cream**

Directions:

Bake pie crust, fitted into a pie tin, for 10 minutes at 450 degrees until lightly browned. Let cool before filling.

Melt chocolate, let cool. Beat together sugar and butter in small mixer bowl using electric mixer for 4 minutes or until light and fluffy. Add cooled chocolate and vanilla to the sugar-butter mixture and beat with electric mixer until blended. Add eggs, one at a time, and beat for 2 minutes after each egg is added. Scoop chocolate filling into the prepared pie crust and spread to fill crust. Beat one cup of cold heavy whipping cream and spread on top of filled pie. Refrigerate until ready to serve.

Cook's Tip!

Brush some beaten egg white over piecrust before baking to yield a beautiful glossy finish.

Peanut Butter Pie

Contributed by Susan Fryer
(Karen's sister)

Ingredients:

Crust:

- **1/2 cup peanut butter**
- **Powdered sugar to make crumbs**
- **1 Keebler chocolate pie crust**

Pie:

- **8 oz. cream cheese, softened**
- **1 cup peanut butter**
- **1 cup sugar**
- **2 cups Cool Whip topping, thawed**

Directions:

Crust: Mix peanut butter and powdered sugar together to make crumb mixture. Sprinkle half of the crumb mixture over pie crust.

Pie: Blend cream cheese and peanut butter, add sugar, blend well. Add Cool Whip and fold into first mixture. Gently spoon mixture over crumbs in crust.

Top with additional Cool Whip and garnish with remaining crumbs.

Keep refrigerated, serve chilled.

Cake Mix Coconut Macaroons

Contributed by Susan Carter

Ingredients:

- **1 Angel Food cake mix**
- **1 egg**
- **2 Tbsp. butter**
- **1/4 cup water**
- **2 cups coconut**

Directions:

Combine all ingredients, and drop by teaspoonfuls onto cookie sheet. Bake at 375 degrees for 8-10 minutes.

Cook's Tip!

To add color to coconut, place in a plastic food container with a few drops of food coloring, snap on the lid, and "shake, shake, shake"!

Pineapple Cream Cheese Dessert

Contributed by Ann Speltz

Ingredients:

- **1-1/2 pkgs. graham crackers, crushed**
- **3/4 stick melted butter or margarine**
- **2 8-ounce pkgs. cream cheese, softened**
- **2 9-ounce containers Cool Whip**
- **1 large pkg. vanilla instant pudding**
- **1 20-ounce can crushed pineapple**

Directions:

Mix graham crackers and butter together and spread in bottom of 9x13 inch baking pan. Bake at 350 degrees for 5 to 8 minutes.

Mix softened cream cheese with juice from pineapple. Beat well with mixer.

Add vanilla pudding mix (dry) and stir in by hand.

Fold in pineapple and Cool Whip and mix well by hand.

Spread over cooled crust and refrigerate until ready to serve.

Apple Crisp

Contributed by Joan Staige

Ingredients:

- **10-12 apples, peeled and sliced**
- **½ cup butter**
- **1 cup sugar**
- **¾ cup flour**
- **1 tsp. cinnamon (heaping)**

Directions:

Put sliced apples in buttered cake pan.

Blend all ingredients until crumbly. Sprinkle over apples.

Bake at 375 degrees for 1 hour.

Easy, Creamy Orange Truffles

Contributed by Susan Carter

Ingredients:

- **1 bag milk chocolate chips**
- **1 can vanilla frosting**
- **1 Tbsp. orange extract**
- **Coconut, cocoa, finely chopped pecan or rainbow-colored sprinkles for rolling and coating truffles**

Directions:

Microwave chocolate chips until melted, stirring occasionally. Stir in frosting and extract. Blend well.

Chill in refrigerator overnight.

Use melon baller or spoon edge to scoop mixture and form into balls. Roll in coating of your choice and place in mini muffin cups.

Makes about 30 truffles.

Chocolate Turtle Cheesecake

Contributed by Linda Grupa

Ingredients:

CRUST

- **1 ½ cups cookie crumbs**
- **3 Tbsp. butter, melted**

FILLING

- **1 (7 ounce) package caramels**
- **¼ cup evaporated milk**
- **¾ cup chopped pecans, divided**
- **2 (3-ounce) packages cream cheese, softened**
- **½ cup sour cream**
- **1 ¼ cups milk**
- **1 (3.9 ounce) package chocolate instant pudding mix**
- **½ cup fudge or caramel topping**

Directions:

Crust: Mix cookie crumbs with melted butter. Press into a 9-inch pie plate. Bake at 350 degrees 6 to 8 minutes.

Filling: Place caramels and evaporated milk in a heavy saucepan. Heat over medium-low heat, stirring continually, until smooth, about 5 minutes. Stir in ½ cup chopped pecans. Pour into crust.

Combine cream cheese, sour cream and milk in a blender. Process until smooth. Add pudding mix; process for about 30 seconds longer.

Pour pudding mixture over caramel layer, covering evenly. Chill, loosely covered, until set, about 15 minutes.

Drizzle fudge topping over pudding layer in a decorative pattern. Sprinkle top of cake with remaining pecans. Chill, loosely covered, until serving time.

Peanut Butter Bars

Contributed by Janet Stanton
(Phil's sister)

Ingredients:

- **1 cup melted butter**
- **1 1/3 cup graham cracker crumbs**
- **4 cups powdered sugar**
- **1 cup peanut butter**
- **12 oz. package of chocolate chips**

Directions:

Mix butter, crumbs, sugar, and peanut butter together in a large bowl.

Melt 12 oz. package of chocolate chips plus 1 tablespoon of peanut butter and spread on top of bars.

Refrigerate if desired.

Cook's Tip!

Short on powdered sugar? Pour granulated sugar into a blender and whir! A half cup granulated makes about one cup powdered.

Pineapple Casserole

Contributed by Lynn Johnson & "Big Jer"
(Phil's cousin)

Ingredients:

- **1 15 ½ or 20 ounce can pineapple tidbits**
- **1 cup sharp cheddar cheese, shredded**
- **¾ cup sugar**
- **3 Tbsp. flour**
- **1 tube Ritz crackers, crushed**
- **1 stick butter**

Directions:

Drain pineapple and place in baking dish. Mix dry ingredients and pour over pineapple. Crumble crackers on top. Drizzle with melted butter.

Bake 40 minutes at 350 degrees.

Auntie Do Do's Raspberry Jell-O

Contributed by Lynn Johnson & "Big Jer"
(Phil's cousin)

Ingredients:

- **2 packages raspberry Jell-O**
- **2 packages frozen raspberries, thawed**
- **2 cups hot water**

Topping:

- **1 cup whipping cream**
- **1 small cream cheese**

Directions:

Mix hot water and Jell-O until dissolved. Mix in thawed berries, including juice. Place in refrigerator until set.

Whip cream and cream cheese together and use as topping.

Peanut Butter Swirls

Contributed by Lynn Johnson & "Big Jer"
(Phil's cousin)

Ingredients:

- **½ cup peanut butter**
- **¾ cup brown sugar**
- **2 eggs**
- **1 cup flour**
- **¼ tsp. salt**
- **1/3 cup margarine**
- **¾ cup sugar**
- **2 tsp. vanilla**
- **1 tsp. baking powder**
- **1 cup chocolate chips**

Directions:

Mix all ingredients – except chocolate chips – until creamy. Pour into greased 9x13 pan. Sprinkle with chocolate chips. Bake at 350 degrees for 5 minutes. Remove from oven and swirl melted chips into bars. Put back in over and bake another 25 minutes.

Cook's Tip!

To determine if an egg is fresh, immerse it in a pan of cool, salted water. If it sinks, it is fresh, but if it rises to the surface, throw it away.

Chocolate Bundt Cake

Contributed by Jody Boughton
(Phil's cousin)

Ingredients:

- **1 pkg. chocolate fudge cake mix**
- **1 pkg. instant chocolate pudding**
- **1 cup (8 ounces) sour cream**
- **½ cup oil**
- **½ cup warm water**
- **4 eggs**
- **1 6-ounce package semi-sweet chocolate chips**

Directions:

Mix all ingredients – except chocolate chips – together. Stir in chips.

Bake in preheated 350-degree oven for 50-60 minutes. Cool.

Cook's Tip!

Best baking pans are thick or insulated and light in color. Dark or nonstick pans absorb heat and can result in burnt, dry baked goods.

Ph'ruit Pizza

Contributed by Jody Boughton
(Phil's cousin)

Ingredients:

Crust:

- **1 ½ cups flour**
- **2 Tbsp. sugar**
- **¾ cup butter**
- **1 cup chopped walnuts**

Topping:

- **8 ounces cream cheese, room temperature**
- **½ cup sugar**
- **1 tsp. vanilla**

Fresh fruits of your choice (i.e., berries, grapes, bananas, kiwi, nectarines, etc.)

Glaze:

- **1/3 cup water**
- **¼ cup sugar**
- **1 Tbsp. corn starch**
- **¼ cup orange juice**
- **1/8 (2 Tbsp.) cup lemon or lime juice**

Directions:

Combine crust ingredients; press into round pizza pan and bake at 350 degrees for 15 minutes. Combine topping ingredients, beat until light and spread onto cooled crust. Arrange fresh fruits on top. Combine glaze ingredients and heat on medium heat until thick. Cool. Pour glaze over fruit layer. Chill.

Chocolate Chip-Malted Milk Cookies

Contributed by Susan Carter

Ingredients:

- **2 3/4 cups flour**
- **3/4 cup plain malted milk powder**
- **1/2 tsp. baking soda**
- **1/4 tsp. salt**
- **1 cup white granulated sugar**
- **1/2 cup brown sugar, firmly packed**
- **1 cup butter, softened**
- **2 large eggs**
- **2 tsp. pure vanilla extract**
- **2 Tbsp. sweetened condensed milk**
- **2 cups milk chocolate chips**

Directions:

Preheat oven to 350 degrees. Combine flour, malted milk powder, baking soda and salt. Mix well and set aside.

Cream sugars and butter in large bowl of electric mixer using medium speed. Add eggs, vanilla and sweetened condensed milk; beat until light and fluffy.

Stir in flour mixture and then chocolate chips until just combined. Do not overmix. If the dough is too sticky to handle, add a little more flour.

Form 1 1/4-inch balls and place onto an un-greased cookie sheet, about 2-inches apart. Bake for approximately 10 minutes, until cookies are slightly brown along the edges. Cool on a cookie sheet for 3 minutes before removing to cooking rack. Makes approximately 4 dozen, 3-inch cookies.

Variation: For a flavor variation, try chocolate-flavored malt powder and change the chips to white chocolate or white vanilla chips. You can also chop up malted milk balls and use instead of the chips, or as a replacement for half the chips.

Beverages, Bits & Tasty Misfits

In assembling this book of contributed recipes, we ended up with a few "leftovers" that just don't seem to fit into any other category, yet certainly deserve to be published.

No problem! We've created a place to put them and call it Beverages, Bits & Tasty Misfits, because they're just too ph'abulous to leave out!

Enjoy!

Bailey's Irish Cream

Contributed by Rose Mary Staige

Mix in Blender:

- **3 eggs**
- **1 can sweetened condensed milk**
- **1 pint half & half (or substitute whipping cream)**
- **1 Tbsp. dry instant coffee**
- **2 Tbsp. chocolate syrup**
- **1 tsp. vanilla**
- **10 oz. brandy**

Store in refrigerator.

Phil's Perfect Bloody Mary Mix (Virgins optional)

Contributed by Phil himsel'ph!

Ingredients:

- **Clamato Bloody Caesar Mix**
- **Wye River Red seasoning**
- **1/2 to 1/2 tsp. horseradish**
- **Vodka (optional)**

Directions:

Fill tall glass with ice and sprinkle seasoning and add horseradish.

Add a shot of vodka and fill glass with Clamato.

Stir to mix well.

Cook's Tip!

Need a cure for headaches? Take a lime, cut it in half and rub it on your forehead. The throbbing will go away.

Grandma Roppes Iced Tea

Contributed by Grandma Roppes
(Phil's grandma)

Ingredients:

- **6 tea bags boiled in one quart water**
- **1 & ½ cups sugar**
- **3 lemons**

Directions:

In a one-gallon jar, pour in the sugar and then pour the hot, strong tea over it.

Add juice squeezed from the lemons and then put in the lemon rinds, too.

Fill the jar ¾ full with water and stir. Pour over ice and enjoy.

Punch

Contributed by Lynn Johnson & "Big Jer"
(Phil's cousin)

Ingredients:

- ***2 cans Hawaiian punch***
- ***1 can lemonade***
- ***1 can orange juice***
- ***3 quarts ginger ale***
- ***1 quart charged water***

Directions:

Mix together, serves 20.

Party Punch

Contributed by Christina Staige

Ingredients:

- **2 packages cherry kool-aid**
- **1 package strawberry kool-aid**
- **2 cups sugar**
- **1 (6 oz.) frozen lemonade**
- **1 (6 oz.) frozen orange juice**
- **1 bottle ginger ale**
- **3 quarts water**

Directions:

Mix all ingredients together except for the ginger ale.

Mix ginger ale in when you are ready to serve. Freeze half of the punch for ice.

*It's best to make two batches, freeze one batch for ice.

Cook's Tip!

Ginger soothes upset stomachs and motion sickness. For a quick cup of ginger tea, add 1 tsp. minced ginger root to 1 cup boiling water and steep 5 minutes. Strain and sip!

Blackberry Wine Cooler

Contributed by Susan Carter

Ingredients for 1 serving:

- **1 Tbsp. blackberry syrup (recipe below)**
- **2 Tbsp. water**
- **1/4 cup dry red wine**
- **1/4 cup sparkling water**

Directions:

Combine ingredients, and serve over ice.

For blackberry syrup:

- **2 cups granulated sugar**
- **1 cup water**
- **2 1/4 cups fresh blackberries or 12 ounce unsweetened frozen blackberries (thawed)**

Stir sugar and water together in saucepan, heat slowly to boiling, lower heat and simmer 5 minutes. Add berries, stir and simmer for 10 minutes more. Cool and strain. Result will be a clear, thin liquid.

Corn and Pepper Relish

Contributed by Sarah Schmanski

Ingredients:

- **2 cups frozen corn**
- **1 red bell pepper, chopped**
- **1 green bell pepper, chopped,**
- **¼ head of cabbage, chopped (about 3 cups)**
- **1 cup cider vinegar**
- **½ cup sugar**
- **½ tsp. each of:**
  - **Turmeric**
  - **Celery seeds**
  - **Mustard seeds**
  - **Salt**

Directions:

Combine corn and the chopped veggies in a bowl.

In a saucepan combine vinegar, sugar, and spices and bring to a boil. Boil for 2 minutes.

Pour boiling liquid over vegetables and stir to combine.

Cool to room temperature and then refrigerate. Stir a few times the first day while it is in the refrigerator.

Keeps fresh forever!

Bev's Beef Jerky

Contributed by Bev Keiper

Ingredients:

- **5 lbs. very lean steak (flank, round, venison, etc.)**

Marinade:

- **½ cup soy sauce**
- **2 Tbsp. worcestershire sauce**
- **½ tsp. of each of the following:**
  pepper,
  garlic powder,
  ground ginger
- **2 tsp. hickory smoked flavored salt**

Directions:

Partially freeze steak to make cutting into strips easier. Slice very thin.

Combine marinade ingredients and marinate for 1 & 1/2 days minimum, turning several times to make sure steak is well seasoned.

Place strips on oven racks (I use refrigerator racks on top of oven racks so smaller pieces don't fall through). I bake two racks at a time.

Bake in 150 degree oven for 6-7 hours, with the oven partially open. I wedge a wooden spoon in the door to keep it slightly ajar.

Jerky (venison or beef)

Contributed by Lynn Johnson & "Big Jer"
(Phil's cousin)

Ingredients:

- **1 ½ lbs. meat**
- **½ cup soy sauce**
- **¼ cup worcestershire sauce**
- **1 tsp. liquid smoke**
- **½ tsp. garlic**
- **1 tsp. Accent**
- **1/3 tsp. pepper**
- **1/3 tsp. salt**

Directions:

Cut meat thin. It will cut easier if meat is partially frozen. Mix remaining ingredients and marinate meat in Ziploc bag for 24 hours in refrigerator. Then put in your dehydrator according to manufacturer's instructions.

Carmel Corn

Contributed by Karen Staige
(Phil's wi'phe)

Ingredients:

- **6-8 qts. popcorn**
- **2 cups brown sugar**
- **2 sticks of butter**
- **1/2 cup corn syrup**
- **1 tsp. salt**
- **1 tsp. baking soda**

Directions:

Preheat oven to 250 degrees.

Pour popped corn onto baking sheets or 9x13 pan.

Combine brown sugar, butter, corn syrup and salt in sauce pan. Bring to a medium boil for 5 minutes, stirring frequently.

Remove from heat and stir in baking soda.

Pour over popcorn and stir to evenly coat.

Bake for 1 hour, stirring every 15 minutes.

Auntie Do Do's Cream Gravy for Lutefisk

Contributed by Jody Boughton
(Phil's cousin)

Ingredients:

- **8 Tbsp. butter**
- **8 Tbsp. flour**
- **1 tsp. salt**
- **2 cups half-and-half**
- **2 cups 2% milk**

Directions:

Melt butter, add flour and bring to a boil. Add salt, cream and milk. Bring to a boil and thicken, stirring constantly; sprinkle with paprika. Pour over Lutefisk and enjoy!

Cook's Tip!

Oops! If you (accidentally) create lumpy gravy, just pour into a blender and whir until smooth again.

Quick and Easy Homemade Jam

Contributed by Susan Carter

Ingredients:

- **1 cup fresh fruit, cubed (strawberries, blueberries, peaches – whatever is in season)**
- **½ tsp. lemon juice**
- **1/8 to ¼ cup apple juice (depending on how sweet the fruit is)**
- **½ to 1 tsp. sugar or sugar substitute**
- **2 tsp. unflavored gelatin**

Directions:

Combine all ingredients in a heavy pot and cook for three or four minutes on high heat. Taste the jam and add more sugar if needed.

Sprinkle one or two teaspoons of unflavored gelatin over the fruit mixture and stir until gelatin is completely dissolved.

Place into container and store in refrigerator. Keeps for several weeks.

Recipes
Ph'rom Ph'amous
People & Places!

Okay, we admit it. The people mentioned in this section aren't exactly close ph'riends, or ph'riends of Phil's ph'riends, or Phil's ph'amily members. But why deprive you of their ph'avorite foods just because they didn't personally send us their recipes?

If you're not lucky enough to live the life of a celebrity, here's your chance to at least taste some of their ph'amily ph'avorites, too!

Tom Cruise's Spaghetti Carbonara

Created by Tom Cruise
As presented on Oprah

Ingredients:

- **1/2 inch of olive oil (for frying pan)**
- **2 cloves of minced garlic**
- **1 chopped onion**
- **8-12 thick slices of Italian bacon (Pancetta; often rolled like a sausage)**
- **4 eggs**
- **2 packages of spaghetti**
- **2 cups grated parmesan cheese**

Directions:

In a frying pan, combine 1/2 inch of olive oil, 2 cloves of minced garlic, one chopped onion and the Italian bacon cut into small squares. Let simmer for about a half-hour, being careful not to let the oil get to a boiling point.

In a bowl, beat 4 eggs with lots of salt and fresh ground pepper.

Bring a pan of salted water to a boil. Cook both packages of spaghetti until al dente, drain and immediately add egg mixture to pasta. The eggs are actually cooked by the pasta. (Make sure the eggs are thoroughly cooked before proceeding.) Stir the egg mixture until it is well mixed. Pour in the mixture from the frying pan and stir. Finish with the parmesan cheese and serve.

Barba Guian (Rissoles) - Appetizer

Contributed by Nick & Lori Edstrom
A Ph'avorite of Prince Rainer, III of Monaco

Pastry:

- **1 ¾ cups flour**
- **7 Tbsp. of butter or margarine**
- **Water and salt**

Mix:

- **Swiss chards, boiled**
- **Minced onion, browned**
- **1 egg**
- **Parmesan cheese**
- **Salt and pepper**

Mix pastry ingredients and roll into a thin sheet. Cut into rounds. Place a teaspoon of filling mix on half the pastry and fold over the other half. Seal edges by brushing with beaten egg yolk. Fry in hot oil, and serve with tomato sauce.

Marinated Steak ala Burt

Contributed by Nick & Lori Edstrom
A Ph'avorite of Burt Reynolds

Marinade for 2 steaks:

- **1 Tbsp. lemon juice**
- **½ cup soy sauce**
- **½ tsp. worcestershire sauce**
- **1 tsp. sugar**
- **½ clove garlic, crushed**
- **2 Tbsp. of your best brandy or bourbon**
- **Dash of liquid red-pepper seasoning**
- **Dash ground ginger**

Directions:

Mix together ingredients for marinade; let steak marinate in this for at least 30 minutes, preferably one hour.

To broil or barbecue steaks, trim excess fat. Slash remaining fat just to the meat (not into it). Place on grill about 4 inches from hot coals to sear. For a 1 ½ inch steak, sear on high, direct heat 3-5 minutes on first side. Turn and cook the other side on medium to low heat.

Cook 5-8 minutes for medium and 12-15 minutes for well done. Since grills and broilers vary, it is best to check doneness by slitting close to the bone or in the thickest part of the meat.

Herb Crispies

Contributed by Nick & Lori Edstrom
A Ph'avorite from the menu of the Pasta Impromptu Restaurant, Barrington, Illinois

Ingredients:

- **½ cup thyme**
- **1 cup oregano**
- **1 quart fresh grated Parmesan cheese**
- **1 cup basil**
- **1 cup parsley**

- **2 & ½ Tbsp. chopped garlic**
- **2 cups butter substitute, melted**

- **2 loaves day old Italian bread, sliced 1/8 inch thick**

Directions:

Mix together thyme, oregano, cheese, basil and parsley. Set aside.

Mix butter substitute and chopped garlic well. With a pastry brush, dab sliced bread with liquid butter mixture.

Generously sprinkle with cheese/herb mixture.

Bake at 350 degrees for 15 minutes or until golden brown.

Serves 15-25

Mom Unser's "Indy" Chili

Contributed by Nick and Lori Edstrom
A Ph'avorite of Marsha and Bobby Unser, professional race car driver

Ingredients:

- **1 lb. lean pork (tenderloin or chops)**
- **1 clove fresh garlic, minced**
- **1 shake oregano**
- **3 cans mild or medium green chilies, chopped**
- **1 medium onion, chopped**
- **1 #2 can of tomatoes**
- **Salt to taste**
- **Pinto beans (optional)**

Directions:

Remove all fat from pork and cut into cubes. Saute pork, onion, and garlic.

Squeeze tomatoes through fingers and add to skillet with tomato juice. Add oregano and salt. Add green chilies and simmer approximately 35 minutes. Add water if necessary.

Add pinto beans, or serve as side dish.

Artichoke Salad

Contributed by Nick and Lori Edstrom
A Ph'avorite at "The Charcuterie at Foley's" restaurant in Dallas, Texas

Ingredients:

- **3 Tbsp. olive oil**
- **3 Tbsp. white wine vinegar**
- **1 Tbsp. minced fresh oregano or 1 tsp. dried**
- **1 Tbsp. minced fresh basil or 1 tsp. dried**
- **1 clove fresh garlic, minced**
- **½ tsp. black pepper**
- **2 cans artichoke hearts, drained and halved**
- **1 green bell pepper, washed, seeded and diced**
- **12 black olives, sliced**
- **12 stuffed green olives, sliced**
- **2 tomatoes, peeled, seeded, cut into julienne strips**
- **Fresh spinach leaves, if desired**

Directions:

Combine olive oil, vinegar, herbs, garlic and pepper to make marinade. Pour marinade over artichokes, cover an refrigerate overnight for 8-10 hours.

One hour before serving, lightly toss marinated artichokes with bell pepper, olives and tomatoes. Let stand at room temperature until serving time.

Serve over fresh spinach leaves, if desired. Serves 8-10.

Broccoli Casserole

Contributed by Nick and Lori Edstrom
A Ph'avorite of Jack Nicklaus, Golf Pro

Ingredients:

- **2 10-ounce packages of frozen chopped broccoli**
- **1 10-3/4 ounce can condensed Cream of Mushroom soup**
- **1 cup mayonnaise**
- **½ cup sour cream**
- **2 Tbsp. onion, grated**
- **1 cup sharp cheese, grated**
- **2 eggs, beaten**
- **Cheese cracker crumbs**

Directions:

Cook broccoli 5 minutes, drain.

Combine soup, mayonnaise, sour cream, onion, cheese and eggs. Add broccoli; put in greased 1-1/2 quart casserole dish. Top with crumbs.

Bake at 400 degrees for 30 minutes.

Note: Best if assembled a day ahead and baked just prior to serving. Do not add crumbs until ready to bake.

Serves 6-8

Seafood Casserole

Contributed by Nick and Lori Edstrom
A Ph'avorite of Yogi Berra, baseball legend and infamous for his slightly skewed "words of wisdom" (see next page)

Ingredients:

- **1 can peeled, chopped tomatoes**
- **3 cloves garlic, minced extremely fine**
- **1 glass white wine**
- **1 handful fresh basil, chopped**
- **½ tsp. thyme**
- **¼ cup olive oil**
- **½ tsp. salt**
- **½ tsp. pepper**
- **Fresh parsley**
- **1 lb. Boston scrod**
- **½ lb. scallops**
- **½ lb. shrimp, peeled**

Directions:

Saute garlic in olive oil, add tomatoes, wine, basil, thyme, salt and pepper, and simmer about an hour. In separate pan, sauté seafood very lightly with fresh parsley. Place seafood in casserole and pour sauce over.

Serve with the crustiest bread you can find to dip in the sauce, and accompany with corn pudding and romaine lettuce salad.

Yogi Berra-isms

As an added treat, here are a few of the sayings that made Yogi so famous ...

"This is like deja vu all over again."

"You can observe a lot just by watching."

"He must have made that before he died."

— referring to a Steve McQueen movie

"You've got to be very careful if you don't know where you're going, because you might not get there."

"I knew I was going to take the wrong train, so I left early."

"If you don't know where you are going, you will wind up somewhere else."

"If you can't imitate him, don't copy him."

"You better cut the pizza in four pieces because I'm not hungry enough to eat six."

"Baseball is 90% mental — the other half is physical."

"It was impossible to get a conversation going; everybody was talking too much."

"A nickel isn't worth a dime today."

"Nobody goes there anymore; it's too crowded."

"I take a two hour nap, from one o'clock to four."

"If you come to a fork in the road, take it."

"You give 100 percent in the first half of the game, and if that isn't enough in the second half you give what's left."

"If the fans don't come out to the ballpark, you can't stop them."

"The other teams could make trouble for us if they win."

"The towels were so thick there I could hardly close my suitcase."

Onions Rozelle (on the barbecue)

Contributed by Nick and Lori Edstrom
A Ph'avorite of Pete Rozelle, National Football League

Ingredients:

- **4 large sweet onions**
- **½ lb. butter**
- **Salt and pepper**

Directions:

Peel onions. Hollow out center of each onion with small knife. Fill center with butter, salt and pepper. Wrap each onion in heavy duty aluminum foil. Put on hot coals for 45 minutes, turning occasionally.

Serve with pork, steak or ribs.

Baja California Chicken

Contributed by Nick and Lori Edstrom
A Ph'avorite of Nancy Reagan, former First Lady

Ingredients:

- **8 boned chicken breasts**
- **4 Tbsp. olive oil**
- **Seasoning salt and pepper to taste**
- **4 Tbsp. tarragon vinegar**
- **2 cloves garlic**
- **2/3 cup dry sherry**

Directions:

Sprinkle chicken with seasoning salt and pepper to taste.

Crush garlic into oil and vinegar in a skillet. Saute chicken pieces until golden brown turning frequently. Remove; place in a baking dish.

Pour sherry over chicken pieces and bake in 350 degree oven for 10 minutes.

Serves 8.

Frank Sinatra's Sauce

Contributed by Nick and Lori Edstrom
A Ph'avorite of Ole Blue Eyes

Ingredients:

- **3 Tbsp. olive oil**
- **½ medium onion**
- **4 cloves garlic**
- **1 large can tomatoes**
- **½ tsp. salt**
- **½ tsp. pepper**
- **¼ tsp. oregano**
- **½ stick butter**
- **Macaroni, cooked**
- **Grated cheese**
- **2 Tbsp. chopped parsley**

Directions:

Brown onion and garlic in oil. Remove garlic.

Drain tomatoes; reserve ¼ cup liquid. Blend tomatoes 4 seconds in a blender; pour into pan and stir. Add the remaining ingredients.

Drain macaroni, add butter and ½ the sauce. Place macaroni on platter, add sauce, cheese and parsley.

Almond Delights

A Ph'avorite of Alec Baldwin, Actor
As presented on the Rosie O'Donnell Show

Ingredients:

- **48 Club crackers**
- **Large bag of slivered almonds**
- **2 sticks of butter**
- **2/3 cups sugar**

Directions:

Preheat oven to 300 degrees.

Line a cookie sheet with foil.

Place crackers, sides touching, in a single layer on the foiled cookie sheet.

Sprinkle liberally with slivered almonds.

Melt butter in saucepan, stir in sugar. When mixture begins to bubble, cook, stirring constantly, for 3 minutes. Pour the butter sugar mixture over the almond/cracker layer.

Bake for 15 minutes – NO LONGER! – and remove promptly.

Cool. Cut. Yum!

Robert Duvall's Mother's Crab Cakes

A Ph'avorite of Robert Duvall, Actor

Ingredients:

- **1 lb. crab meat**
- **2 Tbsp. mayonnaise, heaping**
- **2 eggs, lightly beaten**
- **½ tsp. worcestershire sauce**
- **½ tsp. cayenne pepper**
- **¼ tsp. salt**
- **½ small onion, grated**
- **½ Tbsp. mustard powder**
- **18 Ritz crackers, crumbled**

Directions:

Combine all ingredients, adding the crackers just before forming and sautéing.

Heat frying pan to medium high heat.

Form crab mixture into patties, large for main course, or small for appetizers.

Saute patties, 10 minutes per side until crispy.

Make 6 main course cakes, or 15-19 appetizers.

Macadamia, Chocolate Chip and Peanut Butter Mini-Turnovers

A Ph'avorite of Melanie Griffith, Actress

Ingredients:

- **2 cups smooth peanut butter (room temperature)**
- **½ cup milk chocolate chips**
- **1 cup toasted and chopped macadamia nuts**
- **2 sheets (one package) frozen puff pastry, thawed according to package directions**
- **1 egg, lightly beaten**
- **Confectioner's sugar for garnish (optional)**

Directions:

In large bowl, mix peanut butter, chocolate chips, and macadamia nuts until well combined.

Working with one sheet of pastry at a time, lightly flour a work surface and gently roll pastry in all directions to thin the dough. With a sharp knife, cut the sheet into quarters, then cut each quarter into quarters, to make 16 squares from one sheet of pastry.

Place one teaspoon of filling on the center of each piece of pastry. Fold the pastry on the diagonal to form a triangle. Press edges to complete close filling into pastry. Brush the tops of the turnovers with beaten egg and place on baking sheet.

Bake for 15 minutes. Serve warm, dusted with confectioner's sugar, or as an accompaniment to ice cream.

Makes 32 turnovers.

The Photo Gallery: Phil, Ph'riends & Ph'amily

At first, it was the 'Boys Only' Club ...

Phil is the youngest of the three Staige brothers.

... until the girls showed up!

Phil, John,
Janet, Al & Pat

Phil as:

Horseman

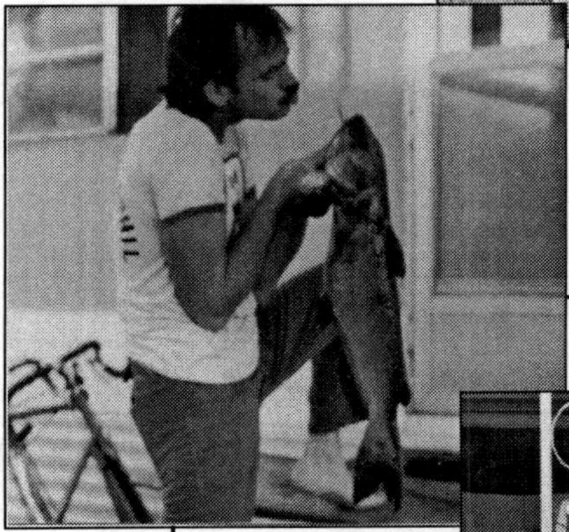

Fisherman

Socialite

Cult Leader
(just kidding ...)

He's been a truck-loving 4-wheeler, on road ...

... and off.

And a law-abiding citizen (except just this once).

This music-loving drummer ...

... was in a Rock 'n Roll Band (Pearl).

Phil met, and married, Karen –

– the love of his life.

And then there were four ...

... first Charlotte, then Katie.

"Staige Struck" ph'amily poses:

Brothers Al, John & Phil

Earl (dad) & Phil

Staige Siblings: Al, Pat,
John, Janet, Phil

A typical family gathering with
Phyllis (mom) at "Center Staige"

Karen, Katie,
Phil, Charlotte

(Ditto!!)

Thank you.

Give-A-Little, Get-A-Lot

Give-A-Little, Get-A-Lot

Give-A-Little, Get-A-Lot

There are thousands and thousands of well-deserving causes begging for your attention and hard-earned cash. Sometimes you can help with a contribution, and sometimes it's just not in the budget. The good news (for us) is that you've already helped the Staige Ph'amily by purchasing this recipe book.

Thank you.

For the movers-and-shakers out there who want to know how else you can help, here are a few 'minimal-time-invested-with-maximum-return' suggestions:

Start An Online Virus (the good kind!)

Do you have an email list of your own ph'amily and ph'riends? Let them know about this cause so that they, too, can "give-a-little and get-a-lot" by trading a few dollars for a fabulous book of recipes. Send an email that directs them to:
http://www.successideas.com/PhriendsOfPhil.htm

Ask for a Little Ink!

If you are a member of an association or club that distributes a newsletter to its members, ask if they would put a small mention of the cause and available recipe book in their next issue. There are short newsletter items already written and available for your use on the Web site at:

http://www.successideas.com/PhilNews.htm

Gift Them To Others

Recipe books make great gifts for cooks, non-cooks, newlyweds and newly independents (like students). Give to your own ph'riends and ph'amily for birthdays, holidays, Mother's Day, wedding showers, anniversaries, and no-particular-reason occasions (discounts available when you buy 5 or more!). You can even package the book with the ingredients or cooking utensils used in your favorite recipe (or package with ready-made treats!) from the book, and give it as a housewarming, hostess or thank-you gift. You'll not only help the Staiges, you'll also be helping your own culinary-challenged ph'riends and ph'amily! There's an order blank on the following page for your convenience.

The Bigger Picture

For opportunities related to joint ventures, retailers, resellers, or corporate sponsorships, please visit the Web site listed below or, to request information by mail, contact Susan at:

Nasus Publishing
P. O. Box 641
Prior Lake, MN 55372
Phone: 952-484-4262
Fax: 925-226-1419
Email: nasuspublishing@successideas.com
Web site: **http://www.successideas.com/PhriendsOfPhil.htm**

How To Order Additional Copies of:

Phil's Ph'riends' & Ph'amily's Ph'avorite Recipes!

1) Online at:

http://www.successideas.com/PhriendsOfPhil.htm

2) By mail:

Copy or clip the order blank below, fill in your information, and send to: **Nasus Publishing, Attn: Phil's Benefit Fund, P.O. Box 641, Prior Lake, MN 55372**

3) **By fax** (VISA and Mastercard orders only):

Fill in the ordering information, and fax to: **925-226-1419**.

- -

Phil's Ph'avorites Order Blank

Name: ______________________________

Address: ______________________________

City: __________________ State: ________ Zip: ___________

Enclosed is: ☐ **Check or Money Order** (Made out to Nasus Publishing)
(check one) ☐ **VISA** charge information
☐ **Mastercard** charge information

Name as it appears on card: ______________________________

Card number: ______________________ Exp. Date: ___________

Card holder verification # from back of card (the last 3-4 digits of the number on your signature line): ________________

	Quantity	Book Price	Shipping	Tax (MN only)	Total
☐	1	$ 17.00 +	$ 2.25 +	$ 1.11	= ______
☐	2 x	$ 17.00 +	$ 3.25 +	$ 2.21	= ______
☐	3 x	$ 17.00 +	$ 4.25 +	$ 3.32	= ______
☐	4 x	$ 17.00 +	$ 5.25 +	$ 4.42	= ______

For orders of 5 or more:

☐	_____ x (enter quantity)	$ 15.00	FREE +	6.5% of total	= ______